CHOCOLATE CANDY

Other books in
The Particular Palate Cookbook™ series

Garlic
by Sue Kreitzman

Ribs
by Susan Friedland

Tailgate Parties
by Susan Wyler

Cookies
by Diane Rozas and Rosalee Harris

Deli
by Sue Kreitzman

Chicken Breasts
by Diane Rozas

Comfort Food
by Sue Kreitzman

CHOCOLATE CANDY

*80 recipes for chocolate
treats from fudge to truffles*

by Anita Prichard

A Particular Palate Cookbook™
Harmony Books/New York

For Frances and Carl, who are truly dedicated chocoholics

A Particular Palate Cookbook

Published by Harmony Books, a division of Crown Publishers, Inc., 225 Park Avenue South, New York, New York 10003

HARMONY, PARTICULAR PALATE, and colophons are trademarks of Crown Publishers, Inc.

Manufactured in the United States of America

Library of Congress Cataloging in Publication Data

Prichard, Anita.
  Chocolate candy.

  "A particular palate cookbook."
  Includes index.
  1. Chocolate candy.   I. Title.
TX791.P888 1985   641.8'53   85-13942
ISBN 0-517-55938-2

10 9 8 7 6 5 4 3 2 1

First Edition

Contents

INTRODUCTION/7

EQUIPMENT/9

INGREDIENTS/13

QUICK-AND-EASY CANDIES/17

TEMPERATURE-CONTROLLED CANDIES/25

CHOCOLATE-DIPPING/45

MOLDING AND DECORATING WITH CHOCOLATE/57

CHOCOLATE TEMPTATIONS/65

SOURCE GUIDE/91

INDEX/93

Introduction

Mention chocolate candy and you'll see eyes light up all around you. Everyone has a favorite kind—but it takes more than an ordinary candy bar to please the refined tastes of today. Chocolate specialty shops or "boutiques" are flourishing, satisfying chocoholics with fancy French truffles in every imaginable flavor from rum to raspberry. But why pay exorbitant prices when you can make professional-quality candies in your own home?

Despite what you may have heard, candy-making is not difficult, but it is exacting. There are a few basic principles that must be followed to ensure success (checking weather conditions and maintaining precise temperatures), but once these are understood, even a beginner can make wonderful chocolate candies. And it doesn't take long to discover just how much *fun* it is to work with chocolate. A lot of candymakers I know do it as a hobby. (They say they like making it better than eating it!)

In my family, chocolate candy has always been a part of our gift-giving at holidays. My mother is still an expert at the age of eighty-six. She turns out a delicious array of old-fashioned holiday candies every Christmas. My own specialty is the art of chocolate-dipping.

Few people of my mother's generation understood the fundamentals of dipping chocolate. I was introduced to the craft as a child when I was granted special permission to watch a very sophisticated lady who lived across town perform her annual Christmas chocolate-dipping ritual. The performance took place out on the rear porch with the lady in question huddled over a pot of melted chocolate, laboriously dipping fondant centers impaled on toothpicks. I'll never forget that sight; it wasn't at all what I expected! But amateurish as the procedure was, I was still duly impressed.

Later when I became seriously involved in candy-making I enlisted the help of my sister, who has a background in chemistry. Together we discovered an easier method for dipping chocolates at home that has been extremely successful. Soon thereafter I had the opportunity to study with Tom Kron, the well-known chocolatier, in his shop on New York's Upper East Side. In my classes I refined a scaled-down version of professional dipping chocolate for the home candymaker who finds it impractical to work with the large quantities used in commercial production. Both these methods are in this book.

For instant gratification, try something quick and easy like the devastingly rich chocolate fudge or chocolate pecan clusters. If you're looking for a passionate, intense chocolate experience, make a tray of rich liquor-flavored truffles. Whatever the chocolate mood of the moment, there's something here for everyone. Homemade chocolate candies are so sinfully sumptuous you'll want to try every recipe.

Equipment

With the exception of a candy thermometer, all of the equipment you need for making candy is probably right in your kitchen. Check to see that you have the following on hand: a set of measuring spoons, graduated liquid and dry measuring cups, a 9 x 12–inch jelly-roll pan, an 11 x 17–inch baking sheet, wire cooling racks, an electric hand mixer, a double boiler, kitchen shears, an 8 x 8 x 2–inch pan, and a 9 x 9–inch shallow pan.

SAUCEPANS A heavy metal pan is a must for making candy. It holds a uniform heat and the candy does not stick or scorch while cooking. Have 1- , 2- , and 3-quart sizes on hand.

SPATULA Use a wide nonflexible spatula with a straight edge. A clean paint scraper may also be used.

THE INDISPENSABLE CANDY THERMOMETER

Accurate cooking temperature is essential at almost every stage of candy-making and chocolate-dipping, and your best tool for the job is a reliable candy thermometer. Veteran candymakers can tell when candy and chocolate is ready by its appearance alone or by its feel, but it takes years of experience to acquire such skills.

I recommend that you use a clearly marked, easy-to-read thermometer with a mercury bulb that is set low enough to measure the temperature of the boiling syrup but does not touch the bottom of the pan, and with clips to hold the thermometer inside the pan while in use. Several such thermometers are available.

Candy Thermometer for Home Use. With a temperature range of 100°F. (38°C.) to 320°F. (160°C.), this thermometer is suitable for everything except tempering chocolate, and can also be used for such noncandies as jellies and frostings. There are several excellent ones available and they come with instructions and a temperature chart on the back of the attached card.

Commercial Candy Thermometer. The temperature range of this is 60°F. (15.5°C.) to 360°F. (182°C.). If you make candy in large quantities for gift-giving or selling, you won't be satisfied with anything but the commercial thermometer by Taylor, which is the one I prefer to use. It costs approximately twice as much as the smaller thermometer, but it is stainless steel and the scale is large and easy to read. It is 12 inches long and therefore not meant for use with small saucepans as its weight could cause a small pan to topple over.

Chocolate-Tempering Thermometer. The temperature ranges from 40°F. (4°C.) to 130°F. (98°C.). A precision instrument such as this makes tempering chocolate easier and more precise. This highly accurate thermometer features a large, easy-to-read scale and can also be used for measuring the temperature of wine, yogurt, or yeast.

To test a candy thermometer for accuracy before using it, put it in a pan of cold water with the mercury bulb completely submerged. Bring the water to a boil and continue to boil for several minutes. The thermometer should register 212°F. (100°C.) at sea level and approximately one degree less for every thousand feet above sea level.

To use a candy thermometer, be sure the thermometer is at room temperature before putting it into hot syrup. Lower the thermometer gradually into the candy mixture *after* the sugar is dissolved and it has started to boil. Be sure the bulb of the thermometer is immersed in the syrup, but be careful to keep the bulb from touching the bottom of the pan. When finished using the thermometer, remove it from the hot syrup and immerse it in hot water for easy cleaning.

When using a candy thermometer at high altitudes, the temperature at boiling point will be below 212°F. Test the thermometer to determine the boiling point and subtract the number of degrees below the 212°F. mark from the cooking temperature in the recipe.

To read a candy thermometer, keep it in an upright position with the mercury bulb completely immersed in boiling syrup. To assure that the thermometer is positioned properly, it is important to use the correct pan size as specified in the recipe. Your eye should be level with the top of the mercury for accurate reading. Do not read the thermometer on a slanted angle or it may show one or two degrees above or below the cooking temperature, which will make a difference in the finished product.

To clean a candy thermometer, use warm, sudsy water. Check carefully to make sure you have removed all sugar crystals. Any crystals left on the thermometer will haunt your next candy-making attempt.

To test without a candy thermometer, use the following procedure. First, remove the candy from the heat. The mixture can change rapidly from one stage to another if it continues to cook while you are testing. Drop a little cooked syrup (about ¼ teaspoon) into a cup of cold but not ice water and quickly pinch the ball between your thumb and forefinger. The following are the cold-water stages:

Soft-Ball Stage (234°F. to 240°F.) For fondant, fudges, and penuches. The syrup forms a soft ball which flattens out between your fingers.

Firm-Ball Stage (244°F. to 248°F.) For caramels, nougat, and divinities. The syrup forms a stiff ball which retains its shape for a minute or two when held between your fingers.

Hard-Ball Stage (250°F. to 266°F.) For molasses, taffy, and soft candies to be pulled. The syrup forms a hard ball which will roll about on a buttered surface when removed from the water.

Soft-Crack Stage (270°F. to 290°F.) For toffee, butterscotch, crunches, and hard candies. The syrup forms spirals or threads which are brittle under water but which soften and become sticky when removed from the water.

Hard-Crack Stage (300°F. to 310°F.) For clear brittle candies, glacées, and some hard candies. The syrup forms spirals or threads which are brittle when removed from the water and do not stick to your fingers.

Caramelized Sugar No cold-water test. The sugar liquefies and caramelizes to a light toast shade. Do not overcook the sugar or it will burn.

DIPPING FORK This is not really a fork but a metal loop fastened at a right angle to a long handle. You can either buy one at a store that sells candy-making equipment or make one yourself.

Use a straight length of copper wire about 10 inches long and heavy enough to shape and bend (coat-hanger wire is too heavy). Make a loop 1½ inches from the end of the wire. Twist the ends tightly to form a circle about ½ inch in diameter; bend the wire at a right angle to form the handle. Do not make the loop too large or your coated centers will slip through it and fall back into the pan.

Or, you can make a dipping fork from an inexpensive two-pronged roasting fork. With pliers, gently bend each prong about 1 inch from the end at right angles to the handle of the fork. This homemade dipper works very well for handling large centers and for caramel-dipping.

Ingredients

First-rate ingredients and accurate measuring can make all the difference in candy-making.

SUGAR *Granulated* is the sugar generally used in candy-making. Granulated and extra-fine granulated can be used interchangeably in the recipes in this book. *Superfine* is a very fine, quick-dissolving granulated sugar. Use superfine in areas of high humidity to help retard excessive crystallization when making cream and hard candies.

Always sift granulated sugar *before* measuring it to remove large grains which will not dissolve properly. Sift the sugar onto wax paper, spoon it into the measuring cup, then level it off with a spatula.

Confectioners' sugar is granulated sugar crushed very fine and mixed with cornstarch to prevent caking. Do not substitute this sugar for granulated in candy recipes. It is important to note whether a recipe calls for the confectioners' sugar to be measured before or after sifting. One cup of unsifted confectioners' sugar will increase to one and one-half cups when sifted.

Light and dark brown sugars are essentially the same, but the light brown has a milder flavor and is used more often for candy. Because brown sugar has a rather high acid content, it usually makes milk or cream curdle at the boiling point. The acidity is needed to produce a creamy candy, so don't worry about the curdling; it will disappear during the final beating. Spoon brown sugar into the measuring cup a little at a time. Pack it down firmly with the back of the spoon. When turned out, it should stand up as if molded.

CREAM OF TARTAR Cream of tartar is used to give some candies a creamier consistency.

BAKING SODA Baking soda combines with the acids in such candy ingredients as honey and brown sugar to produce a gas that causes brittles and crunches to separate into layers. Measure both cream of tartar and baking soda very carefully; too much of either one will add unwanted flavor to the candy and make it heavy and difficult to cream in the final beating.

BUTTER The recipes in this book were tested with Land O' Lakes unsalted butter. If possible, always use a top-grade unsalted butter for a fresh and delicate flavor. Do not substitute whipped butter for regular butter in candy recipes, because the density is different.

CHOCOLATE OR COCOA Always use a premium-quality chocolate or cocoa as called for in a recipe. Substituting one for the other changes the results and affects the flavor.

CORN SYRUP Corn syrup, called glucose by professionals, is used extensively in candy-making because it prevents candy from getting grainy. Do not substitute dark corn syrup when the recipe calls for light.

MOLASSES AND SORGHUM These can be used interchangeably in candy recipes.

HONEY Honey used in candy-making is the liquid type.

HEAVY CREAM Known as whipping cream in some localities, heavy cream is 35% to 40% butterfat. This produces the richest candy. *Undiluted evaporated milk* can be substituted for heavy cream.

LIGHT CREAM Light cream, or coffee cream, contains 18% to 20% butterfat and produces a candy slightly less rich than heavy cream does.

HALF-AND-HALF OR WHOLE MILK You can substitute equal amounts of diluted evaporated milk or light cream in any recipe that calls for half-and-half or whole milk. Do not use *skimmed milk* because it does not contain enough butterfat.

DRIED SKIMMED MILK SOLIDS When mixed with water, skimmed milk solids can replace milk in recipes, but you must add 2 tablespoons of unsalted butter per cup of water.

NUTS *To roast nuts,* leave them in the largest possible pieces. Unless otherwise specified in a recipe, place the nuts—blanched or unblanched—in a 300°F. oven and turn them frequently with a wooden spoon to avoid scorching. Most nuts, except pecans and walnuts, improve the taste of candy if they are very lightly roasted first to bring out their rich flavor. Remember, when roasted nuts are added to brittles, crunches, and toffees, the high temperature of the cooked syrup will continue to roast them.

An alternate method for roasting almonds and hazelnuts requires perfect oven temperature control. Preheat the oven to 350°F. Place the nuts in the oven and immediately turn off the heat. Set a timer for 15 minutes. Do not open the oven. Remove the nuts from the oven immediately. They will be lightly roasted and perfect for candy-making.

To chop nuts, use a chef's knife, a hand grater, or a blender. To chop nuts in a food processor, use the metal blade. A shredding disk will also chop nuts to a fine, uniform texture, but not as fine as when they are chopped with a metal blade. Chop up to 2 cups of nuts at a time, and always chop nuts *after* they have been roasted. Process with on-and-off pulses, checking frequently to avoid the stage where the nuts become oily.

To blanch nuts, pour boiling water over them before shelling and let them stand for 1 minute at the most. Longer soaking will waterlog the kernels. Some shelled nuts have a thin inner lining of skin. Drain the nuts and pinch off the skins. Spread the nuts on a baking sheet to dry.

To remove skins from roasted peanuts, filberts (hazelnuts), and pistachio nuts, wrap them in a terrycloth towel while they are still warm and rub them around until friction loosens the skin.

To store or freeze nuts, leave them in their shells and place them in airtight plastic bags. Store them in the freezer or in a cool place. Light, heat, moisture, and exposure to air tend to make shelled nuts rancid. Difficult nuts, like pecans and Brazil nuts, should be shelled before they thaw completely. Be sure to discard any kernels that are shriveled or dry; they will add a bitter or rancid taste to the candy. Shelled nuts can be kept up to 2 months at 70°F., and as long as 2 years in the freezer. Whole nuts yield about 1 cup of nut meats per pound.

COCONUT *To prepare fresh coconuts,* pierce the eyes with a screwdriver. Drain off the liquid and heat the coconut in a 350°F. oven for 15 to 30 minutes, or until the coconut is cracked. Tap all over with a hammer, then break the coconut open. Pry out the meat and pare off the dark skin. To grate the meat, use a hand grater, blender, or food processor.

To toast coconut, spread grated coconut on a baking sheet. Bake in a 350°F. oven for about 15 minutes or until light brown, stirring frequently.

To tint coconut, mix a few drops of food coloring with a few drops of water in a glass jar. Add approximately 1 cup of grated coconut and shake until evenly colored.

To freeze coconut, grate it first, then pack into containers, allowing a 1-inch space at the top for expansion.

STORING AND FREEZING CHOCOLATE CANDY

Homemade candy keeps well for 2 or 3 weeks if properly stored in airtight containers in a cool, dry place at about 65°F.—never in the refrigerator or in direct sunlight. Candy can be made ahead of time; in fact, some types need a day or two to ripen, or mature, to bring out their best flavors. Still, it is well to keep in mind that freshness is one of the reasons most people enjoy homemade candy and confections.

Candies are generally divided into two categories: the creamy confections and the brittle, crackly, crystalline ones. Do not store brittle candies in the same container with soft, creamy candies because the moisture from the softer candy may make the hard candies sticky.

Wrap all caramel before storing to prevent spreading. Keep chocolate and other hand-dipped candies in crinkle cups, or use some other means of keeping them from touching each other, and store in single layers (I use plastic trays that meat is packaged on) until time to arrange gift-box assortments. Never pile coated candies in plastic bags because this will damage the gloss.

All candies will keep almost indefinitely in the freezer if properly wrapped in airtight freezer bags or containers. Candies may be dipped in coating and gift-boxed before being frozen. Double-bag the box to eliminate the slightest possibility of an air leak.

To thaw candy, let it stand for several hours or overnight and come to room temperature *before* opening containers or bags. This prevents moisture from collecting on candies due to a change in temperature. This is especially important if the candies are to be dipped in chocolate coating. If the candies have *already* been coated with chocolate, they should *never* be taken out of the freezer container or bag until they have thawed completely. This will take 5 to 6 hours. Removing them too soon will cause gray streaks to form on the coating from the sudden temperature change, and all your best efforts will be ruined.

CANDIED FLOWERS Candied rose petals, violets, mimosa, and mint leaves can be purchased in gourmet food stores and make attractive candy decorations.

FOOD COLORINGS FDA-certified food colors come in three forms—liquid, powder, and paste. Liquid colors are good for most candy-making because the shades remain pastel. If a brilliant shade is desired (as for marzipan), use paste or powder colors. (See Source Guide, page 91.) The colors listed below are available already mixed, or you can make them at home by blending the four basic colors.

Liquid coloring is measured in drops from the bottle; paste and powder colorings are measured in "toothpick" quantities—that is, the amount that will cling to the tip of a toothpick.

Color	Number of Drops			
	Red	Yellow	Green	Blue
Orange	1	3	•	•
Rust	3	3	•	•
Lavender	1	•	•	2
Purple	3	•	•	1
Olive green	•	2	3	•
Lime	•	6	1	•
Brown	3	2	2	•
Raspberry	8	•	•	1
Strawberry	7	1	•	•

FLAVORINGS There is a wide range of pure flavoring extracts and oils available. Do not use imitation flavors because they give an off-taste to the finished candy. (See Source Guide, page 91.) Generally a quarter-teaspoon of oil is equivalent to one teaspoon of flavoring extract. Use flavoring oil if you want a strong, concentrated flavor—for example, in such candies as fondant and marzipan.

THESE FLAVORS ARE COLORED AS FOLLOWS:

Anise . . . . .Pink
Apricot . . . . .Pale orange
Banana . . . . .Yellow
Black walnut . . . . .Light brown
Butter rum . . . . .Yellow-brown
Butterscotch . . . . .Yellow
Cherry . . . . .Red
Cinnamon . . . . .Red
Clove . . . . .Gold or red
Coconut . . . . .White
Lemon . . . . .Yellow
Licorice . . . . .Black
Lime . . . . .Yellow-green
Maple . . . . Brown
Orange . . . . .Orange
Peppermint . . . . .Pink or white
Pineapple . . . . .Light yellow
Raspberry . . . . .Blue-red
Spearmint . . . . .Green
Wintergreen . . . . .Pale green or pale pink

Quick-and-Easy Candies

NEVER-FAIL FUDGE

Recommended as Centers for Chocolate Coating

This is a foolproof recipe that turns out right in any kind of weather—wonderfully smooth and dense. Unsweetened chocolate is used to give a bitter edge to the finished fudge. If you prefer your fudge on the sweeter side, use semisweet chocolate bits.

Makes 1 ¼ pounds

1 ⅔ cups granulated sugar
⅔ cup light cream or ⅔ cup (1 small can) evaporated milk, undiluted
6 squares (6-ounces) unsweetened chocolate, chopped, or 1 six-ounce package semi-sweet chocolate bits
1 ½ cups miniature marshmallows

1. Combine the sugar and light cream or milk in heavy 2-quart saucepan and cook over medium heat, stirring constantly with a wooden spoon, until the sugar is dissolved and the mixture comes to a boil. Boil, stirring constantly, for 5 minutes.

2. Remove from heat and quickly blend in the chocolate and marshmallows with a wooden spoon.

3. Stir until thick; pour into an 8 x 8 x 2-inch pan lined with buttered foil.

4. Cool until firm.

5. Turn out onto a smooth surface and cut into 1-inch squares. If the fudge is to be dipped in coating, cut into ½-inch squares.

SPIRITED FUDGE In Step 4, add 2 tablespoons Cognac, flavored brandy, rum, or liqueur of your choice.

COCONUT FUDGE In Step 4, add 1 cup lightly toasted coconut.

CHOCOLATE MINT FUDGE Use mint-flavored chocolate bits. In Step 4, add 2 tablespoons crème de menthe or a few drops of oil of peppermint.

CHOCOLATE NUT CLUSTERS

This easy-to-make, fudgy-textured candy is delicious, and the recipe may be doubled or tripled.

Makes about 50 one-inch clusters

1¼ cups (8 ounces) semisweet chocolate bits *or* 1 cup semisweet chocolate bits plus 2 ounces (2 squares) unsweetened baking chocolate for richer chocolate flavor
⅔ cup sweetened condensed milk
¾ cup lightly roasted nuts, any kind

1. Melt the chocolate in the top of a double boiler over hot, not simmering, water. Stir until smooth.

2. Remove from the heat and blend in the condensed milk and nuts.

3. Drop the mixture by teaspoonfuls onto baking sheets lined with waxed paper.

4. Cool the clusters by placing them in the refrigerator for 15 minutes and then letting stand at room temperature for 2 to 3 hours or until firm.

ORANGE-WALNUT CHOCOLATE CLUSTERS In Step 2, use chopped walnuts and ¼ teaspoon oil of orange.

COCONUT-RAISIN CHOCOLATE CLUSTERS In Step 2, omit the nuts and add ½ cup flaked coconut and ½ cup raisins.

IF IT SAYS "CHOCOLATE FLAVORED"

All chocolate is manufactured according to established world standards. American chocolate must also meet the federal government standards of identity for chocolate. But according to both sets of standards, a product called "chocolate"—be it unsweetened, semisweet, sweet, or milk chocolate—may not contain any vegetable fat other than cocoa butter. Check the ingredients listing on the label to be sure you've got the real thing.

There are some solid and semiliquid products that are generically termed "sweet chocolate and vegetable fat coatings." Technically, these are chocolate-*flavored* products.

AMARETTO BALLS

Recommended as Centers for Chocolate Coating

Serve these confections in lieu of after-dinner liqueurs.

Makes 36 one-inch balls

2 ½ cups (about 75) vanilla wafers, crushed
1 cup confectioners' sugar (measure before sifting)
½ cup lightly roasted blanched almonds, chopped
2 tablespoons Dutch-process cocoa
3 tablespoons light corn syrup
¼ cup Amaretto or other almond-flavored liqueur
confectioners' sugar for coating

1. Combine the crushed wafers and 1 cup sugar in a large mixing bowl.

2. Add the almonds and cocoa and stir well with a wooden spoon.

3. Add the corn syrup and Amaretto and continue stirring until well mixed.

4. With your hands, shape tablespoons of the mixture into 1-inch balls. Roll each ball in confectioners' sugar and place on a baking sheet to dry for several hours.

5. Store the balls in an airtight container for 2 to 3 days to "age." They may be frozen up to 6 months.

PEANUT RUM BALLS In Step 2, substitute roasted unsalted peanuts for the almonds. In Step 3, substitute dark rum for the Amaretto.

CHOCOLATE MARSHMALLOWS

Recommended as Centers for Chocolate Coating

Marshmallows should be firm on the outside but soft when you bite into them. For some unexplainable reason, certain brands of pure vanilla extract will cause the candy mass to literally collapse, resulting in a foamy mass of marshmallow cream. As long as I use the A&P brand of pure vanilla extract, I never have any problems. If that is unavailable, substitute almond extract or some other flavoring.

Makes 64 one-inch squares

4 teaspoons unflavored gelatin
⅓ cup cold water
½ cup granulated sugar
⅓ cup Dutch-process cocoa
⅔ cup light corn syrup
½ teaspoon vanilla or almond extract
½ cup confectioners' sugar sifted with ½ cup cocoa

1. Put the gelatin into a small heavy saucepan. Add the cold water and stir well with a wooden spoon to dissolve. Let stand for 5 minutes, until the mixture becomes firm.

2. Liquefy the mixture over low heat.

3. Combine the granulated sugar, cocoa, corn syrup, dissolved gelatin, and flavoring in a large mixing bowl.

4. Beat on high speed for 15 minutes—no cheating! The marshmallow mixture will be very thick and fluffy.

5. Lightly butter an 8 x 8 x 2-inch pan and sprinkle liberally with the combined confectioners' sugar and cocoa mixture.

6. Pour the marshmallow mixture into the prepared pan. Smooth the top surface with a spatula and sprinkle with more of the combined sugar and cocoa. Place in the refrigerator overnight or for several hours to firm.

7. Remove from refrigerator and, with a spatula, loosen the sides and bottom of the marshmallow square, keeping it in one piece.

8. Turn out onto a baking sheet coated with more of the sugar-cocoa mixture. The marshmallow will be rather sticky until thoroughly coated.

9. Dip a pair of kitchen shears in cold water and cut the marshmallow into 1-inch squares.

10. Roll each piece in the sugar-cocoa coating and place on a rack to dry for several hours. They will stay moist in an airtight container for approximately 3 weeks.

TOASTED COCONUT MARSHMALLOWS Omit the sugar-cocoa mixture. Instead, lightly butter the pan and coat the bottom with 1 cup lightly toasted flaked coconut. Pour in the marshmallow mixture and sprinkle 1 more cup of lightly toasted coconut on the top surface. When firm, cut into 1-inch squares and coat the sides with additional toasted coconut.

CRÈME DE MENTHE MARSHMALLOWS Omit the vanilla or almond flavoring and substitute peppermint extract or a few drops of oil of peppermint and add a few drops of green food coloring.

VANILLA MARSHMALLOWS Omit the cocoa. Combine ½ cup confectioners' sugar sifted with ½ cup cornstarch for coating. The marshmallows may be tinted any desired color. Any flavoring may be used. (See coloring and flavoring charts, page 16.)

CUTTING AND SHAPING MARSHMALLOWS
Marshmallow chicks, bunnies, and eggs are favorite Easter candies. To make your own, prepare several batches of marshmallow, and add desired flavoring and coloring. Use cookie cutters dipped in cold water if you do not feel adept at cutting free forms. Roll each form in the coating as soon as it is shaped and place it on a rack to dry. The forms may be dipped in Chocolate Coating. They are also very colorful if rolled in tinted sugar sprinkles.

MARSHMALLOW CANDY BARS Prepare the marshmallow mixture. Cut the firmed marshmallow into bars 1-inch wide and 2 ½-inches long. Roll the bars in the coating and dry them on a rack overnight. Shake off excess coating and dip in chocolate. The chocolate-coated bars may then be garnished with nut halves, chopped nuts, or coconut.

THE FIRST CANDY

The ancient Egyptians were the first to make candy by mixing honey with fruits and spices. Around the eleventh century, Arabs learned how to process sugar and used it to make sweet confections. When fourteenth-century Crusaders came back to England from the Holy Land, they used the word *qand* to describe the sweets they brought home. *Qand* quickly became *candy* and has been satisfying sweet tooths ever since.

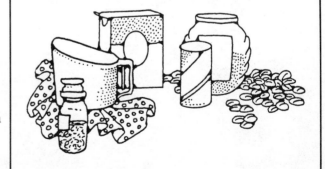

GRAND MARNIER BALLS

Recommended as Centers for Chocolate Coating

These confections provide a piquant contrast with a cup of good tea. They also make a gift to delight any connoisseur of sweets.

Makes 60 one-inch balls

1 cup butterscotch bits
½ cup granulated sugar
3 tablespoons light corn syrup
½ cup Grand Marnier or other orange-
     flavored liqueur
2⅔ cups (about 85) vanilla wafers, crushed
1 cup pecans or walnuts, finely chopped
confectioners' sugar for coating

1. Melt the butterscotch bits in the top of a 1-quart double boiler over hot but not simmering water, stirring with a wooden spoon until smooth.

2. Add the sugar, corn syrup, and Grand Marnier. Continue stirring until blended.

3. In a large mixing bowl combine the crushed wafers, pecans or walnuts, and butterscotch mixture. Mix well with a wooden spoon.

4. With your hands, shape tablespoons of the mixture into 1-inch balls. Roll the balls in confectioners' sugar and place them on a baking sheet to dry for several hours.

5. Store them in an airtight container for 2 to 3 days to "age." They may be frozen up to 6 months.

ORANGE BALLS In Step 2, substitute ½ cup undiluted frozen orange juice concentrate for the Grand Marnier.

Temperature-Controlled Candies

Temperature-controlled candies, sometimes referred to as boiled-sugar candies, are classified as either cream or hard candy. These candies are easy to make but if your previous candy-making efforts were unsuccessful, even though you followed recipe instructions to the letter, the weather was most assuredly the culprit. Low humidity and high barometric pressure are the two essential weather conditions necessary to reduce the moisture content enough to crystallize the sugar syrup and firm the finished candy.

An unwrapped piece of hard candy left at room temperature on a rainy or humid day quickly becomes a sticky mess because the sugar in the candy has absorbed the moisture in the air. The same thing happens to the boiling syrup during the cooking process. Even though the candy is cooked to the correct temperature, it will absorb moisture from the air during the beating process, resulting in a runny mass that never firms up. Low humidity in the 20% to 40% range is ideal for successful candy-making. In an air-conditioned room the humidity will be a few degrees lower.

When cooking fudge-type candies, if the humidity percentage is marginal (55% to 65%) the candy will firm easier when the ingredients are cooked at two degrees higher than the temperature recommended in the recipe. Adjusting the temperature will compensate for the moisture in the air. The cooking of divinities, fondant, nougats, and those candies made with honey, molasses, or applied glazes should *never* be attempted unless the humidity is in the 20% to 40% range.

Candy will *not* get firm, regardless of the amount of humidity in the air, unless the barometer reads 30 inches or higher. A barometer is an instrument used to measure atmospheric pressure, which is a good indicator of approaching weather changes. If the barometer reads 30 inches and falling, this means a storm system is approaching and the making of candy is risky business. If you think the weather may not be conducive to candy-making, call your weather bureau for the percentage of humidity in the air and the barometric pressure reading.

FUDGE-MAKING BASICS

1. Watch the temperature! When fudge reaches the boiling point, the mixture becomes very sensitive to jarring, stirring, or beating, and increases in sensitivity as the temperature rises. If the fudge curdles during the cooking process, keep calm. Curdling means that the acid of the chocolate is reacting properly with the milk or cream. Jarring, stirring, or beating the syrup before it has cooled to 110°F. will cause sugar crystals to form, making the candy coarse and grainy. Attempts to speed cooling usually complicate the procedure. If you can't wait for it to cool, "paddle out" the fudge as in the Professional Method on page 28.

2. Fudge changes in appearance during the beating process. It will be glossy and thin at first. As the beating continues, the gloss will gradually disappear until, quite suddenly, the mixture starts to thicken. Drop a small quantity from a spoon onto a piece of waxed paper. If it holds its shape, the beating is done.

3. Don't be discouraged if your fudge hardens in the pan before you can turn it out. This can happen to the most accomplished fudge-maker. Just scrape the whole mass onto a baking sheet, as in the Professional Method (below), and knead it, while it is still warm, into a delectable creamy confection.

4. Prepare the lightly oiled pans or molds while the candy is cooling to the temperature recommended for beating.

5. Spread the fudge to a depth of ½ to ¾ inch and, when partially cooled, cut it into ½- to 1-inch squares using a warm knife coated with butter.

Professional Method Professional chocolatiers use this method, sometimes called "paddling out," to cream fudge into soft centers for dipping in chocolate, summer, or soft caramel coatings. This method eliminates beating and sudden hardening of the candy that may occur during the beating process.

1. Have a baking sheet with sides and a wide spatula on hand. Prepare the fudge as the recipe directs, cooking the syrup to the recommended soft-ball stage (page 10). Quickly run the baking sheet under cold water and shake off any excess moisture. Place the dampened sheet over a wire cooling rack.

2. Holding the saucepan down close to the surface, slowly pour the hot syrup in a steady stream onto the baking sheet, jarring the mixture as little as possible. Do *not* scrape the pan.

3. Add the butter to the syrup mixture, but *do not* stir.

4. Cool for 10 to 12 minutes, or until luke-warm. Test by placing the palm of your hand underneath the baking sheet. If it feels only slightly warm, the mixture is ready to be worked with a spatula.

5. Add any flavoring. Work the spatula back and forth, keeping the entire mass in motion, until the candy begins to thicken and loses its gloss. As soon as this happens, spread the candy into a rectangle.

6. Cut the fudge into squares using a large knife coated with butter, or press it into lightly oiled molds. Fudge can also be cut or kneaded into many creative shapes, and when it is slightly warm it will remain creamy long enough to be cut with cookie cutters.

ROYAL CHOCOLATE FUDGE

This rich chocolate fudge will delight the most discriminating chocoholic. The recipe makes a large quantity and can easily be halved.

Makes 3 pounds

2 cups granulated sugar, sifted
1 cup light brown sugar, firmly packed
1 tablespoon (¼ ounce) unflavored gelatin
1 cup milk
½ cup light corn syrup
5 squares (5 ounces) unsweetened chocolate, chopped
1 cup (2 sticks) unsalted butter, cut in 1-inch slices
2 teaspoons vanilla extract

1. Combine the sugars, gelatin, and milk in a heavy 3-quart saucepan; blend well with a wooden spoon. Stir in the corn syrup, chocolate, and butter.

2. Start the syrup boiling and clip on the candy thermometer.

3. Cook over medium heat, stirring frequently, until the thermometer registers 234°F. Then stir constantly because the mixture has a tendency to scorch. Move the thermometer around the sides of the pan until the temperature reaches 239°F. or the syrup forms a soft ball (page 10) in cold water.

4. Remove from heat and pour onto a baking sheet with sides. Cool for 10 minutes.

5. Add the vanilla and start working the mixture with a wide metal spatula as in the Professional Method (page 28) for handling fudge. When the fudge starts to thicken and mold up on the back side of the spatula, spread it into an 9 x 12-inch foil-lined pan. Cool until firm and use as desired.

CHOCOLATE FUDGE

Recommended as Centers for Chocolate Coating

The amount of unsweetened chocolate used in the following recipe depends upon individual taste. The fudge will be very dark and densely flavored if you use 3 squares (3 ounces) of chocolate.

Makes 64 one-inch pieces

2 to 3 squares (2 to 3 ounces) unsweetened chocolate, chopped
⅔ cup half-and-half or light cream
2 cups granulated sugar, sifted
2 tablespoons light corn syrup
⅛ teaspoon salt
2 tablespoons unsalted butter
1 teaspoon vanilla extract

1. Lightly oil the sides of a heavy 2-quart saucepan.

2. Add the chocolate and half-and-half. Cook over low heat, stirring constantly with a wooden spoon until the mixture is smooth.

3. Stir in the sugar, corn syrup, and salt. Continue stirring with the wooden spoon over low heat until the sugar is dissolved. You should not be able to feel sugar grains when you rub the spoon against the sides of the saucepan. Do not let the mixture come to a boil.

4. Remove from heat and, with a damp paper towel or small sponge, wipe the sugar grains above the liquid level from the sides of the pan.

5. Start the syrup boiling and clip on the candy thermometer.

6. Cook over medium heat, without stirring, until the thermometer registers 236°F. or the syrup forms a soft ball (page 10) in cold water.

7. Remove from heat and add the butter. Cool, without stirring, until the mixture is lukewarm (110°F.).

8. Add the vanilla and beat vigorously with a wooden spoon until the mixture begins to thicken and lose its gloss.

9. Quickly spread the fudge into a lightly oiled 8 x 8 x 2-inch pan. Cool until firm.

10. Cut into 1-inch squares. If the fudge is to be dipped in coating, cut into ½-inch squares.

CHOCOLATE FRUIT FUDGE Add ½ to 1 cup of chopped dried fruit such as dates, figs, raisins, or candied cherries at the end of Step 8.

CHOCOLATE NUT FUDGE Add ½ to 1 cup unsalted almonds, filberts, peanuts, hickory nuts, or walnuts at the end of Step 8. Lightly roasting the almonds, filberts, or peanuts will improve the flavor.

CHOCOLATE COCONUT FUDGE Add ½ to 1 cup fresh or commercially prepared shredded or grated coconut at the end of Step 8. If fresh coconut is used, be sure it is thoroughly dried before adding it to the candy or the fudge will be too soft. Fresh coconut can be dried by placing it on a baking sheet in an oven at low heat for a few minutes.

MARSHMALLOW FUDGE Add 1 cup miniature marshmallows at the end of Step 8.

CHOCOLATE ALMOND BUTTER FUDGE Substitute ¼ cup almond butter for the unsalted butter. Omit the vanilla and substitute ½ teaspoon almond extract. Do not stir until the mixture has cooled to lukewarm (110°F.)

CHOCOLATE PEANUT BUTTER FUDGE Substitute ½ cup creamy peanut butter for the unsalted butter. Do not stir until the mixture has cooled to lukewarm.

CHRISTMAS FUDGE Add 1 cup miniature marshmallows, ½ cup lightly roasted pistachio nuts, and ½ cup candied cherries, quartered, at the end of Step 8.

BOURBON FUDGE CLUSTERS

These candies are perfect for gift-giving because they pack and ship very well if wrapped individually in aluminum foil or waxed paper.

Makes 60 clusters

2 cups granulated sugar, sifted
6 tablespoons Dutch-process cocoa
¾ cup cold water
½ cup unsalted butter
½ teaspoon almond extract
2 tablespoons bourbon
1 cup pecan or walnut halves

1. Lightly oil the sides of a heavy 2-quart saucepan.

2. Add the sugar, cocoa, water, and butter.

3. Cook over low heat, stirring constantly with a wooden spoon, until the mixture is smooth and the sugar is dissolved. You should not be able to feel sugar grains when you rub the spoon against the sides of the saucepan. Do not let the mixture come to a boil.

4. Remove the mixture from the heat and, with a damp paper towel or small sponge, wipe any sugar grains above the liquid level from the sides of the pan.

5. Start the syrup boiling and clip on the candy thermometer. Cook slowly after the mixture starts to boil until the thermometer registers 234°F. or the syrup forms a very soft ball (page 10) in cold water. Do not stir during the cooking process.

6. Remove from heat and, without stirring, cool to lukewarm (110°F.).

7. Add the almond extract and bourbon and beat vigorously with a wooden spoon until the mixture begins to thicken and lose its gloss.

8. Quickly drop the mixture by teaspoonfuls onto waxed paper and top with a pecan or walnut.

CHOCOLATE PRALINES

These candies are made from a fudge mixture which is beaten as soon as it is removed from the heat and dropped like cookie dough into 2-inch round patties.

Makes 24 pralines

2 to 3 squares (2 to 3 ounces) unsweetened
    chocolate, chopped
1 cup light brown sugar, firmly packed
1 cup granulated sugar, sifted
½ cup milk or light cream (cream will
    produce a richer confection)
2 tablespoons unsalted butter
1 cup pecan halves

1. Lightly oil the sides of a heavy 2-quart saucepan.

2. Add the chocolate, both sugars, and the milk or cream. Cook over low heat, stirring constantly with a wooden spoon, until the sugar is dissolved. When you rub the spoon against the sides of the saucepan, you should not be able to feel sugar grains. Do not let the mixture come to a boil.

3. Remove from heat and, with a damp paper towel or small sponge, wipe any sugar grains above the liquid level from the sides of the pan.

4. Start the syrup boiling and clip on the candy thermometer.

5. Cook over medium heat, without stirring, until the thermometer registers 236°F. or the syrup forms a soft ball (page 10) in cold water.

6. Remove from heat and add the butter and pecans. Start beating immediately using a wooden spoon and continue until the mixture is just slightly thick and begins to cloud. Do not overbeat or the pralines will not spread.

7. Quickly drop the mixture by heaping tablespoons onto lightly oiled baking sheets. Cool until firm.

CARAMEL-MAKING BASICS
1. Do not make caramels on a damp or humid day.
2. Caramels have a tendency to scorch on the bottom of the pan, so stir the mixture often while cooking.
3. Lightly butter or oil the cooling pan, or the finished caramel will be too greasy.
4. Caramels, if they are not to be coated with chocolate, must be cut and wrapped after they are cool to prevent them from spreading.
5. To wrap caramels, cut waxed paper or plastic wrap into sizes just large enough to fold over the top and across the ends of each one.
6. Stored in an airtight container in a dry, cool place, they will keep up to 6 weeks.

CHOCOLATE CARAMELS

Recommended as Centers for Chocolate Coating

Using sweetened condensed milk in this confection makes it quick and easy to prepare. The result is a sinfully rich chocolate caramel, ready in just 30 minutes.

Makes 80 one-inch caramels

1 cup unsalted butter
2 ¼ cups granulated sugar, sifted
2 squares (2 ounces) unsweetened chocolate, chopped
¼ teaspoon salt
1 cup light corn syrup
1 ⅓ cups (1 fourteen-ounce can) sweetened condensed milk
½ teaspoon vanilla extract
1 cup chopped pecans or walnuts (optional)

1. Melt the butter in a heavy 2-quart saucepan over low heat.

2. Add the sugar, chocolate, and salt and stir with a wooden spoon until thoroughly blended.

3. Add the corn syrup and, stirring constantly, gradually add the milk.

4. Start the mixture boiling and clip on the candy thermometer. Cook over moderate heat, stirring as often as necessary to prevent scorching, until the thermometer registers 248°F. or the syrup forms a firm ball (page 10) in cold water.

5. Remove from heat and let stand for 5 minutes. Add the vanilla and optional nuts.

6. Quickly spread the mixture into a lightly oiled 9 x 9 x 2-inch square pan.

7. When it has cooled to room temperature, turn the block of candy out onto a smooth surface.

8. Cut into 1-inch squares with a large sharp knife. (To dip in chocolate coating, cut into ¾-inch squares and dip as soon as possible.)

9. Immediately wrap each *uncoated* caramel in waxed paper or plastic wrap.

SOFT CARAMEL

This is a superb melt-in-the-mouth caramel that can also be used for coating candies and other confections. I used this caramel, pecans, and dipping chocolate to simulate the famous "turtles," which firmly established my reputation as a candymaker.

Because this caramel is very soft, you will have a hard time cutting it into squares. I recommend dropping the warm caramel in little round patties from the tip of a teaspoon onto a lightly oiled baking sheet. When the rounds have cooled to room temperature, they can be dipped in chocolate coating.

Using the correct size saucepan for this recipe is important. I find that a 1-quart size that measures about 5½ inches across the bottom is ideal. With this size pan, the total cooking time will be approximately 1 hour and 20 minutes.

Makes 2 cups

1 cup granulated sugar, sifted
⅔ cup light corn syrup
¼ teaspoon salt
¼ cup unsalted butter

1½ cups whole milk
½ teaspoon vanilla extract

1. Put the sugar, corn syrup, and salt in a heavy 1-quart saucepan. Cook over low heat, stirring constantly with a wooden spoon, until the sugar is dissolved. Do not let the mixture come to a boil. When you rub the spoon against the sides of the saucepan you should not be able to feel sugar grains.

2. Start the syrup boiling and clip on the candy thermometer.

3. Cook slowly, without stirring, until the thermometer registers 248°F., about 4 to 5 minutes, or until the syrup forms a firm ball (page 10) in cold water.

4. Add the butter and stir with a wooden spoon until melted. Then stir continuously while adding ½ cup milk and cook again to 248°F. Then stir in another ½ cup milk and recook to 248°F.

5. Add the last ½ cup milk and stir often over moderate heat until the thermometer registers 240°F. or the syrup forms a soft ball (page 10) when dropped in cold water. (This high-low or "slacking back" cooking process of adding the milk in three equal portions produces a particularly soft and butter-rich coating. During the final cooking, do not panic if the mixture seems to be browning too much. This is the normal caramelizing of the syrup and gives the candies their delicious flavor.)

6. Remove the mixture from the heat and cool down to 145°F. Stir in the vanilla. Reheat slowly if the mixture becomes too cool for dipping or coating.

CHOCOLATE CARAMEL ROUNDS For perfectly formed rounds, drop the warm caramel from the tip of a teaspoon onto a lightly oiled baking sheet, holding the spoon close to the baking sheet. Cool to room temperature and coat with chocolate.

APRICOT CARAMELS

Recommended as Centers for Chocolate Coating

These tart-sweet candies may be cut and wrapped as with Chocolate Caramels. But they are especially delicious if you take the time to dip them in a rich chocolate coating.

Makes 64 one-inch caramels

2 cups granulated sugar, sifted
1 cup milk
¼ teaspoon salt
3 cups dried apricots, finely chopped
1 tablespoon unsalted butter
½ teaspoon almond extract

1. Lightly oil the sides of a heavy 2-quart saucepan.

2. Add the sugar, milk, and salt. Stir with a wooden spoon, over low heat, until the sugar is dissolved. When you rub the spoon against the side of the saucepan, you should not be able to feel sugar grains.

3. Remove from heat and, with a damp paper towel or small sponge, wipe any sugar grains above the liquid level from the sides of the pan.

4. Start the syrup boiling and clip on the candy thermometer.

5. Cook over medium-low heat, stirring occasionally, until the thermometer registers 240°F. or the syrup forms a soft ball (page 10) in cold water.

6. Add the apricots and boil the mixture, stirring constantly, until the candy has recooked to 230°F.

7. Remove from heat and add the butter. Beat vigorously until the mixture starts to cool.

8. Add the almond extract and continue beating until the mixture starts to leave the sides of the pan. Quickly spread into a lightly oiled 8 x 8 x 2-inch pan.

9. Cut into 1-inch squares. If the candy is to be dipped in coating, cut into ½-inch squares.

TOFFEE

This soft, crunchy toffee is excellent when dipped in chocolate coating. If desired, a thin layer of Soft Caramel (page 35) may be spread over the toffee before it is cut into squares.

Makes 100 to 120 pieces

1 cup unsalted butter
1 cup granulated sugar, sifted
⅓ cup light brown sugar, firmly packed
2 tablespoons water
½ teaspoon baking soda
½ cup filberts, lightly roasted and chopped
   (optional)

1. Melt the butter in a heavy 2-quart saucepan over low heat.

2. Add the sugars and water. Cook over low heat, stirring constantly with a wooden spoon, until the sugars are dissolved and the mixture comes to a boil. Clip on candy thermometer and continue to cook over low heat, stirring constantly. To prevent separation of butter and sugar, keep the mixture boiling until the thermometer registers 280°F. or the syrup forms a soft-crack ball (page 10) in cold water.

3. Remove from heat; quickly stir in the baking soda and blend thoroughly. Stir in the optional nuts.

4. Immediately pour into a lightly oiled 8 x 8 x 2½-inch square pan.

5. With a knife, make deep indents to mark ½-inch squares.

6. When cold, turn out onto a smooth surface and break the pieces apart.

TOFFEE- AND CRUNCH-MAKING BASICS

1. The fat content is high in both toffee and crunch, so there is no danger of crystallizing the candy by overstirring during the cooking process.

2. Nuts can either be added to the cooked syrup just before it is poured into the pan or be placed in the pan first and the cooked syrup poured over them. If you choose the latter method, the nuts must be very lightly roasted as explained on page 14.

3. Because of the high fat content, both toffee and crunch will keep in the refrigerator or freezer almost indefinitely. Store the candies in airtight containers in layers separated by sheets of waxed paper.

CHOCOLATE ALMOND BUTTER CRUNCH

Almond butter is a wonderful new product distributed by the Almond Board of California. It has the consistency of peanut butter, but contains less fat. Butter must be added to obtain the desired crunchiness and rich flavor.

Makes 80 pieces

¾ cup almonds, lightly roasted and finely ground
1 cup almond butter
2 tablespoons unsalted butter
1 cup granulated sugar, sifted
⅓ cup light corn syrup
⅓ cup water
1 cup semisweet chocolate bits or melted chocolate coating

1. Sprinkle ¼ cup of the almonds evenly onto the bottom of a lightly oiled 9 x 9 x 2-inch square pan.

2. Heat the almond butter and unsalted butter in the top of a double boiler over simmering water and keep warm until the candy syrup is cooked.

3. Lightly oil the sides of a heavy 2-quart saucepan.

4. Add the sugar, corn syrup, and water. Cook over low heat, stirring constantly with a wooden spoon, until the sugar is dissolved. When the spoon is rubbed against the sides of the saucepan, you should not be able to feel sugar grains.

5. Remove the syrup from the heat and, with a damp paper towel or small sponge, wipe any remaining grains above the liquid level from the sides of the pan.

6. Start the syrup boiling and clip on the candy thermometer.

7. Cook over low heat, without stirring, until the thermometer registers 305°F. or the syrup forms a hard-crack (page 10) in cold water.

8. Remove from heat, add the almond butter mixture, and stir until thoroughly blended. Pour at once into the prepared almond-lined pan. Spread to an even depth with a spatula.

9. Let cool for 5 minutes. Then quickly sprinkle the chocolate bits over the candy. The heat will melt the chocolate. Using the spatula, spread the chocolate evenly over the crunch. Sprinkle on the remaining almonds and press down lightly.

10. With a knife, make deep indents to mark 1-inch squares. When the crunch is cool, turn it out onto a smooth surface and break the pieces apart.

CHOCOLATE MAPLE CREAMS

Recommended as Centers for Chocolate Coating

If your particular chocolate passion is delicately flavored maple cream, try this very reliable recipe. This fondant is softer than Chocolate Fondant and must be cooked to a slightly higher temperature. Form in small ovals, dip in rich chocolate, and top with a walnut or pecan half.

Makes about 80 pieces

¾ cup water
2 cups granulated sugar, sifted
⅔ cup pure maple syrup
1 teaspoon vanilla extract

1. Lightly oil the sides of a heavy 2-quart saucepan.

2. Add the water, sugar, and maple syrup. Follow Steps 2 through 6 from Chocolate Fondant (page 40).

3. Cook over low heat, without stirring, until the thermometer registers 240°F. or the syrup forms a soft ball (page 10) in cold water. Continue to follow the steps for Chocolate Fondant through Step 11. Add the vanilla extract while working the fondant, in Step 10.

AMBROSIA FOR THE GODS

When the Greek gods on Mount Olympus sat down to dine on ambrosia, it is possible that what they actually ate was a sweet candy brittle made with honey. The real mystery of ambrosia is hidden in the Olympian clouds, but mythology tells us that, in addition to being an aid to immortality, it was "nine times as sweet as honey"—which aptly describes honey boiled down to a brittle.

CHOCOLATE FONDANT

Recommended as Centers for Chocolate Coating

Most cookbooks recommend cooking fondant syrup to 238°F., but increase the temperature just one more degree and the candy mass will be much more manageable.

Makes 100 to 110 small centers

1⅓ cups water
3 cups granulated sugar, sifted
5 teaspoons Dutch-process cocoa
¼ teaspoon salt
⅓ cup light corn syrup

1. Lightly oil the sides of a heavy 3-quart saucepan.

2. Add the water, sugar, cocoa, salt, and corn syrup. Cook over low heat, stirring constantly with a wooden spoon, until the sugar is dissolved. When you rub the spoon against the sides of the saucepan, you should not be able to feel sugar grains. Do not let the mixture come to a boil.

3. Remove from heat and, with a damp paper towel or small sponge, wipe any remaining grains above the liquid level from the sides of the pan.

4. Return the mixture to moderate heat. Cover the pan long enough for the mixture to boil, which should take 2 or 3 minutes—no more!

5. Uncover the pan and wipe the sides again to remove any stray sugar grains. This step is a must.

6. Start the syrup boiling again and clip on the candy thermometer.

7. Cook over low heat, without stirring, until the thermometer registers 239°F. or the syrup forms a soft ball (page 10) in cold water.

8. Remove from heat and pour the mixture in a slow, steady stream onto a large damp baking sheet with sides. *Do not* scrape the pan.

9. Cool to lukewarm (110°F.). The bottom of the baking sheet should feel just warm, not hot.

10. Work the fondant with a wide spatula by lifting and folding the edges of the candy mass toward the center. When the candy loses its translucency and begins to become opaque, gather it into a ball and knead it with buttered hands. Stop as soon as the mass is smooth and creamy and the ball holds together, or it may become too soft.

11. Wrap the fondant ball in plastic wrap and store it in the refrigerator in an airtight container. The candy must ripen for a minimum of several hours but preferably for 2 or 3 days.

COFFEE MOCHA FONDANT Substitute 1 ⅓ cups strong black coffee for the water.

VANILLA FONDANT Omit the cocoa. In Step 10, add 1 teaspoon vanilla extract.

FONDANT-MAKING BASICS Fondant is a thick, creamy sugar paste used in making chocolate-coated creams, mint patties, and many other melt-in-your-mouth candies. The object is to produce a creamy mass in which the sugar grains are of the smallest possible size.

1. Very dry, cool weather, with the barometric pressure above 30 inches and steady, is essential for successful fondant-making (page 27).

2. Measure ingredients and follow recipe instructions carefully, paying close attention to the details that explain how to handle the candy mass.

3. Even experienced cooks sometimes cook fondant until it is too hard to knead into the desired creamy mass. If this happens, wrap the fondant in a steaming hot terrycloth towel which has been wrung out. Then cover the wrapped ball with a large mixing bowl and let it stand for about 15 minutes. This will soften the fondant so it can be kneaded.

4. Wrap the fondant in plastic wrap and store it in an airtight container to age for several hours at least (2 to 4 days is better). Most fondants can be stored in the refrigerator for 10 days, provided the container is airtight, or in the freezer for up to 2 months.

5. If the fondant is too soft to form good centers (overkneading or lengthy storage may cause this problem), knead a small amount of confectioners' sugar into it. This will make the fondant firmer, though somewhat coarser and less creamy.

CHOCOLATE DIVINITY

Recommended as Centers for Chocolate Coating

Traditionally, these candies are not coated. I discovered they are less sweet if a pecan or walnut half is placed on the mound of candy before it firms and just the bottom is dipped in a coating of very rich, dark chocolate. See page 50.

Makes 35 to 40 pieces

⅔ cup light corn syrup
½ cup water
2⅓ cups granulated sugar, sifted
¼ teaspoon salt
¼ cup egg whites (whites from 2 large eggs)
½ cup Dutch-process cocoa
½ teaspoon vanilla extract
1 cup lightly roasted pecans or walnuts,
    coarsely chopped (optional)

1. Lightly oil the sides of a heavy 2-quart saucepan.

2. Add the corn syrup and water. Cook over moderate heat until the mixture boils.

3. Remove from heat and add the sugar and salt.

4. Return to heat and stir with a wooden spoon until the sugar grains are dissolved. When you rub the spoon against the sides of the saucepan, you should not be able to feel sugar grains. Do not let the mixture come to a boil.

5. Remove from heat and with a damp paper towel or small sponge, wipe any remaining grains above the liquid level from the sides of the pan.

6. Return the mixture to moderate heat, and cover the pan long enough for the mixture to boil, which should take 2 or 3 minutes—no more!

7. Uncover the pan, remove from heat, and with a damp paper towel or small sponge again wipe the sides of the pan above the liquid level to remove any stray sugar grains.

8. Start the syrup boiling again and clip on the candy thermometer. Cook over medium-low heat, without stirring, until the thermometer registers 265°F. or the syrup forms a hard-ball (page 10) in cold water.

9. Begin beating the egg whites when the candy is almost cooked so the syrup will not have time to cool. Beat until very stiff and continue beating while adding the cooked syrup in a slow, steady stream. *Do not* scrape the pan. Add the cocoa and vanilla and continue beating until the candy loses its gloss and retains its shape when a sampling is dropped from a spoon onto waxed paper.

10. Remove the beaters and blend in the optional nuts with a wooden spoon.

11. Drop by teaspoonfuls onto a waxed paper–lined baking sheet. When the candy has cooled, store it in an airtight container.

COFFEE MOCHA DIVINITY Substitute strong black coffee for the water.

CHRISTMAS DIVINITY Omit the cocoa. Increase the vanilla to 1 teaspoon. Add ½ cup chopped candied cherries. Use lightly roasted slivered almonds or pistachio nuts in place of walnuts or pecans.

ORANGE DIVINITY Omit the vanilla and substitute 3 tablespoons finely grated orange rind.

DIVINITY-MAKING BASICS To create this light-as-air relative of a classic Italian meringue, sugar, water, and corn syrup are boiled to the firm- or hard-ball stage (page 10) and the hot syrup is slowly beaten into stiffly beaten egg whites. Individual mounds of candy are dropped from the tip of a teaspoon onto waxed paper or the mixture is poured into a lightly oiled pan and cut into squares.

1. A word of truth is better than a ruined batch of candy. The word is *weather.* At least one day of very dry, cool *weather,* with the barometric pressure above 30 inches, should precede the making of this candy (page 27).

2. Do not double the recipe. Beating can be difficult if the recipe is too large.

3. Separate the eggs as soon as you remove them from the refrigerator. Place the whites in a large mixing bowl and let them come to room temperature before beating.

4. Don't worry if the first portion of the syrup becomes hard when mixed with the egg whites. The heat will soften the mixture as more syrup is added.

5. If making individual mounds, work quickly when dropping the candy from a teaspoon or the mixture will harden in the bowl.

6. Divinities, like meringues, are perishable if exposed to the air. Store them in an airtight container in a cool, dry place.

Chocolate-Dipping

There is nothing more rewarding in candy-making than dipping your own chocolate. Mastering the technique takes some practice, but nothing will impress your guests and friends more than an appealing selection of chocolates dipped by your own hand.

CHOCOLATE-DIPPING BASICS Choose a clear, cool, dry day to dip chocolates.

The work area should be large enough to hold a tray of centers to be dipped on one side and a baking sheet lined with waxed paper for the dipped chocolates on the other side. Always keep the area free of steam and cooking vapors, and avoid drafts.

Have on hand the following equipment: a thin 1-quart metal double boiler (do not use ceramic or glass); a wide rubber spatula; a 2-cup measuring cup; a grater; an instant-reading thermometer; and two baking sheets lined with waxed paper.

Summer coating, chocolate, and water do not mix. Water thickens both summer coating and chocolate, and even a tiny drop will cause trouble. When testing the temperature of the water in the bottom of the double boiler, be extra careful not to let any droplets fall into the melting mixture. Any moisture from the air or steam from the double boiler will make the mixture crumbly and impossible to handle, and the chocolates will dry with gray streaks.

Centers for Dipping Individual recipes in this book give instructions for forming centers for dipping. Nuts, dried fruits, and pretzels are easier to dip than cream centers, so if you're a beginner, practice with these until you have mastered the necessary hand control. With a little practice you will soon progress to dipping soft-cream centers, marshmallows, Easter eggs, and fresh fruit.

1. All fondants must be made at least 2 days before dipping. This allows the moisture to dry out. Regardless of how "well-tempered" your chocolate may be, excess moisture in the centers can cause "bloom" (a dusty gray surface) on the finished chocolates. If the centers are freshly made when you coat them, the bottoms will leak within a few hours.

2. All centers should be room temperature before dipping. Do not dip chilled centers because they will cool the chocolate mixture too fast and cause gray streaking. Centers that are too warm will thin out the chocolate.

3. Keep centers uniform in size and not too large—not more than 1 inch in diameter. The chocolate coating will increase their size.

HOT TRAYS

The Salton Hotray with *variable temperature control* is highly recommended for someone who frequently works with chocolate. It will keep chocolate and summer coating at the proper temperature for dipping and molding. Turned to the lowest setting, the temperature control knob will maintain a constant low heat. All you need to do is place the tempered chocolate or summer coating in a flat-bottomed pan, such as the top of a double boiler, set it on the glass-topped tray and proceed with the dipping. Do not attempt to use a Hotray or any other electric heating unit that doesn't have variable heat controls; the single-temperature models get too hot.

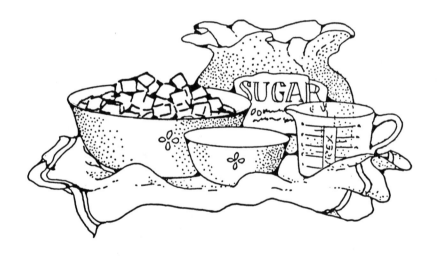

EASY-METHOD CHOCOLATE-DIPPING

This revolutionary method for hand-coating professional-quality chocolates is especially recommended for beginners. With a few simple kitchen tools and two readily available ingredients, you will soon be able to make extravagant-looking confections. Custom-blending your own mixture will enable you to make batch after batch of firm, glossy milk or dark chocolates without the slightest blemish or gray streak to betray the amateur hand.

Ingredients

You may have been warned *not* to combine real chocolate with summer coating, but I have had success with this method for fourteen years and I can assure you the result will taste better than most of the "real chocolates" being sold in fancy shops.

Use unsweetened (baking) chocolate. The most readily available is Baker's, which comes in 8 one-ounce squares to a package. Many brands are available, but each one is slightly different in flavor. My preference is Bissinger, but it is a matter of personal taste. Just be sure to use a rich, natural chocolate that is made from ground cocoa beans and contains cocoa butter. Read the list of ingredients carefully. If vegetable shortening is included in the ingredients, do not use it. The cocoa butter is what gives the finished chocolates a glossy sheen and mouth-watering rich taste. I do not recommend the use of sweet or semisweet chocolate because it will make the finished coating too sweet. Combining sweetened chocolate and summer coating will also cause the finished chocolates to develop "bloom," a dusty gray surface.

The other ingredient is summer (white) coating. There are various brands available. To avoid confusing summer coating with white chocolate—and often people selling the products do not know the difference—I recommend two readily available brands. One is Wilton Enterprise's Candy Melts (wafers), and the other is White Coating Wafers,

---

AN EARLY TECHNIQUE

At the end of the nineteenth century a gift of hand-dipped chocolates became a symbol of love and thoughtfulness. But try as they might, home candymakers were unable to produce professional-looking chocolates. The authors of early cookbooks attempted to solve the problem with the following advice: "Melt 1 block paraffin (5-cent size), add 12 ounces of chopped sweetened chocolate, and melt." Adding paraffin to stabilize the chocolate mixture and add gloss to the finished chocolates was a technique used by candymakers until recently.

packed by Maid of Scandinavia Co. (See the Source Guide, page 91.) Summer coating stabilizes the chocolate mixture, which means that the cocoa butter does not separate from the rest of the ingredients, causing those hateful gray streaks and spots. Do *not* substitute white chocolate, or you will have nothing but trouble. White chocolate will cause spots and streaks in the candies.

Preparation of the Chocolate Coating

Both chocolate and summer coating melt faster and have more sheen when finely grated. You can do this by hand, or with a Mouli grater for small amounts. For larger quantities I use my Oster Food Crafter. A food processor can be used to finely chop the summer coating, but it will not grate, or flake, the chocolate.

When hand-grating, be sure the grater is completely dry. Handle both as little as possible to prevent them from absorbing moisture from your hands, and work quickly. Hand-grating chocolate is a pesky chore because the flakes tend to fly around. It helps to place the grater in or over a large bowl. Do *not* use an electric blender, because the motor shaft will melt the chocolate prematurely and gray streaks will appear in the final product.

The selection of milk, dark, or bittersweet chocolate coating does not necessarily depend on the center. This is very much a matter of individual taste. Normally, the sweeter the center, the darker the chocolate coating.

You can vary these proportions to taste, but don't use less than 1 cup summer coating to 3 cups chocolate, or the mixture will harden too fast and require frequent reheating. Do not use less than 4 cups of dipping mixture or you will not have enough coating in the pan to dip and cover the centers. See the delicious recipes for using end-of-the-pan coating on page 54.

One-quarter pound summer coating or unsweetened chocolate equals 1 cup finely grated.

Milk Chocolate Coating Mixture. Use 3 cups grated or finely chopped summer coating and 1 cup grated unsweetened chocolate.

Dark Chocolate Coating Mixture. Use 2 cups grated or finely chopped summer coating and 2 cups grated unsweetened chocolate.

Bittersweet Chocolate Coating Mixture. Use 1 cup grated or finely chopped summer coating and 3 cups grated unsweetened chocolate.

1. Put the grated summer coating in the top half of a double boiler and put water in the lower half. Do not let the top half touch the water. Heat the water to 140°F. stirring the summer coating continuously with a wide rubber spatula until melted.

2. Remove the pan of summer coating and place the candy thermometer in the hot water. Maintain the water temperature at about 140°F.

3. Continue to stir the summer coating while off the heat until the mixture has cooled to lukewarm (110°F.). The bottom of the pan should be just barely warm to the touch.

4. Add grated chocolate, 1 tablespoon at a time. Stir continuously with a rubber spatula, keeping all the mixture in motion. Stirring helps homogenize and blend the cocoa butter and ensures a rich, glossy sheen on the finished chocolates. If the mixture starts to stiffen, reheat it in the double boiler for a few seconds—just long enough to melt the chocolate. Again, be careful of moisture falling into the chocolate mixture. The longer you stir the mixture, the more gloss your chocolates will have when they dry. *Do not beat* the mixture or you will have air bubbles on the surface of the finished chocolates.

5. Cool the mixture down to about 90°F., stirring constantly with a rubber spatula. After the melted chocolate coating is thoroughly blended, place a lid over the *bottom* part of the double boiler containing the hot water and set it on a low heat so you can use it for reheating. Keep stirring the chocolate mixture until it is cool to the touch. It will look something like thick chocolate pudding, and a string of chocolate about 1½ inches long will dangle from the end of the rubber spatula. Start making little dabs of chocolate on a separate piece of waxed paper. The chocolate is at the correct temperature for dipping when the samples dry and gloss over in about 1½ minutes.

6. Leave the rubber spatula in the pan and place the melted chocolate in the middle of the prepared work area. Stir the chocolate mixture occasionally during the dipping process.

Hand-Dipping Procedure

Hand-dipping is done directly from the pan. If you've used a dipping fork in the past, you will soon learn that hand-dipping solves a lot

of problems. First, it is much easier to control the temperature by actually getting the "feel" of the mixture. Second, the excess coating that causes heavy bottoms on chocolates dipped with a fork, can be controlled by rapping your fingers against the side of the pan.

It may be necessary to reheat the dipping mixture. The mixture should remain at the dipping temperature (90°F.) for 20 to 25 minutes, depending on the weight of the metal in the double boiler, the temperature of the room, and how much "swishing" around of the chocolate mixture takes place during the actual dipping. The warm water in the bottom of the double boiler is less dense and cools faster than the thick chocolate mixture. Therefore, after the chocolate mixture has cooled and become too thick for hand-dipping, it may be necessary to reheat the

CHOCOLATE-COATED FRUIT

Chocolate-coated fruit is very much in vogue. Either the Easy-Method mixtures (page 50) or Professional Dipping Chocolate (page 55) may be used for this purpose.

Have ready an assortment of luscious red strawberries, seedless orange sections, dried apricot halves, glacéed Australian apricots, dried pear halves, and pitted dates. Fresh fruit must be free of moisture. Leave the fruit at room temperature for several hours to dehydrate the dipping surface.

Work as quickly as possible and dip either the whole fruit or the tip of the fruit into the tempered chocolate and place on a waxed paper–lined baking sheet to firm. Since fresh fruits are perishable, dip them the day they are to be eaten.

water before reheating the chocolate mixture. There is no limit to how many times the mixture can be reheated. Just take care that the temperature does not go over 110°F. If the chocolate is melted at too high a temperature, it will not melt smoothly and will produce a grainy, streaked coating.

1. With palm facing you, hold up the middle and index fingers of the right hand in a V (for Victory) sign. Enclose the thumb and the rest of the fingers. The two extended fingers form the V for your dipping fork.

3. Place the right hand, formed in the V dipping position, into the chocolate mixture and roll the center around to coat it.

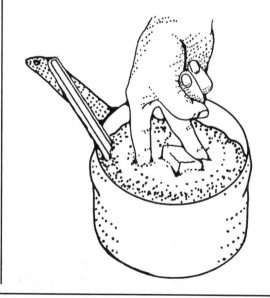

2. Throughout the dipping process the left hand must be kept clean and free from chocolate so you can use it to decorate the chocolates with nuts, coconut, etc. Using your left hand, drop a center from the tray on the left side of your work area into the chocolate.

4. With the fingers still in the V position, palm side up, scoop up the coated center. It will have a lot of extra chocolate sticking to it. With the coated center resting firmly in the fork formed by the fingers, gently rap the backs of the fingers on the edge of the pan to shake off the excess chocolate.

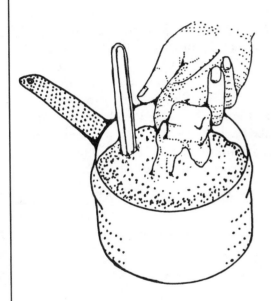

5. Turn the coated chocolate over onto the tray lined with waxed paper on the right side of the work area. Be careful not to slide the center around once you have set it down, or the chocolate will be wiped off the bottom.

6. If the center does not drop easily because of stickiness, manipulate it with the middle finger until it is resting against your thumbnail, then push it off onto the waxed paper with your thumb.

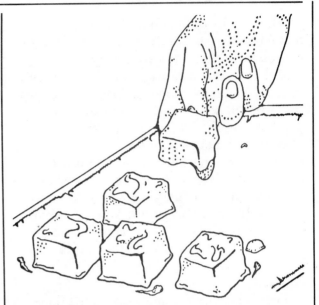

7. After the coated center is placed on the waxed paper, lift your middle finger straight up, pulling a string of chocolate that you can use to make a design on top. Or, if the chocolate is the right temperature, you can pick up a string from the pot and use that to make a design.

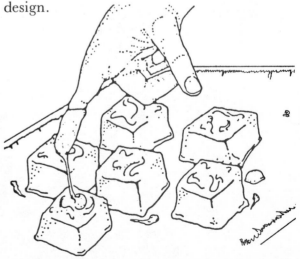

53

After all the centers have been dipped, touch up any bare spots using a bit of warm chocolate on the end of your finger.

If the weather conditions are favorable, by the time you have dipped a dozen chocolates the first will be dry and nicely glazed over. If you have finished dipping and your chocolates are still not glazing over, put the trays of dipped chocolates into the refrigerator for 2 or 3 minutes. Remove them quickly or they will sweat and the moisture will create gray streaks. If your chocolates have gray streaks despite all your best efforts, convert them into French creams by redipping and rolling them at once in ground nuts or unsweetened cocoa.

Leave the coated centers on waxed paper for several hours, until the bottoms are thoroughly dry. If they are removed too soon, the chocolate may stick to the waxed paper and candies with soft centers will develop leaks.

To use up leftover dipping chocolate, remelt the chocolate and mix in nuts, raisins, toasted coconut, chopped dried fruits, etc. Drop the mixture from a teaspoon onto waxed paper. Don't be surprised if you get a lot of requests for these tasty end-of-the-pot creations.

Chocolate Almond Bark Stir ¾ cup lightly roasted almonds into 1 cup leftover melted chocolate. Using a wide spatula, spread the mixture on a clean baking sheet to a depth of about ¼ inch. Cool until firm. Break into bite-size pieces. To make the chocolate look more like bark, score it with a fork before it sets. Any kind of nuts, or a combination of nuts and raisins, can be substituted.

PROFESSIONAL CHOCOLATE-DIPPING

In recent years high-quality ready-made dipping chocolate or "couverture" has become available in many supermarkets and specialty shops. Working with this expensive product can be a great challenge for the home candymaker who is preparing small amounts of chocolate to be melted and maintained at the recommended dipping temperature.

Ingredients

Quality chocolate coating is determined by the amount of cocoa butter it contains. The brand you buy is strictly a matter of taste. Generally speaking, the more expensive the chocolate, the more cocoa butter it contains. If you are serious about becoming proficient with chocolate, I suggest you experiment with 1- and 2-pound amounts before you buy chocolate in quantity. Do *not* attempt to blend your own mixture, using several name brands. Each brand and type of chocolate melts within a slightly different temperature range. Listed are name brands sold in four types—white chocolate, milk, semisweet, and bittersweet chocolate—which I have used with much success. Try Bissinger's, Calle-baut, Carma, Ghirardelli, Guittard, Lenotre, Lindt, Sarotti, Suchard, and Tobler. This list is not exhaustive; there are many more manufacturers of fine chocolate coating.

Do not use semisweet chocolate bits. These morsels are formulated to retain their shape in baking; therefore, it is almost impossible to melt them at the low temperatures recommended for professional chocolate dipping.

It is important to know whether the chocolate you have purchased is "tempered" or "untempered" chocolate. Tempered chocolate has a high satin gloss without any gray streaks running through it when you break off a piece. Untempered chocolate has lost its gloss and has "bloom" on the surface and gray streaks running throughout. All premium-quality chocolate leaves the manufacturer in "temper." If the chocolate is not stored properly it will become untempered, giving it an unattractive appearance, but in no way does this affect the quality. Chocolate which has lost its temper must be remelted at a higher temperature than chocolate in good temper.

Preparation of Chocolate Coating

Allow yourself 45 to 60 minutes for the tempering procedure. Chocolate should be heated and cooled very slowly to allow the mixture to stabilize, which gives the chocolate a nice gloss after the coating has firmed.

1. Determine if the chocolate is "tempered" or "untempered."

2. Chop the chocolate into small (¼-inch) pieces, using a chef's knife or food processor. Do not use less than 1 pound of chocolate—2 or more pounds is better.

3. Put the chopped chocolate in the top half of a double boiler; set aside. Fill the lower half of the double boiler with very warm water. Tap water heated to 140°F. will be about the right temperature.

4. Off the stove, place the top half of the double boiler containing the chocolate over the hot water. It will be necessary to keep changing the water to maintain this temperature. Do not attempt to reheat the mixture by placing the double boiler on the stove. Stir constantly with a rubber spatula; scrape down the sides of the pan frequently so that the chocolate heats evenly: to 115°F. for tempered chocolate coating; 120°F. for untempered chocolate coating; or 110°F. for tempered white chocolate coating. Use your instant thermometer to keep the mixture at the recommended temperature.

5. Immediately remove the chocolate from over the hot water. Stir constantly—do not beat—until the chocolate cools to 79°F. for milk chocolate and white chocolate coating, or 82°F. for dark chocolate coating. Do *not* attempt to lessen the cooling time by placing the mixture over ice water.

6. Stir the mixture gently a few times so it will heat evenly. Off the stove, rewarm the chocolate over hot water to 88°F. to 91°F. for dark chocolate, or 84°F. to 87°F. for milk chocolate and white chocolate coating. Do *not* let the temperature go above 92°F. or fall below 77°F. If this should happen, repeat the tempering process from Step 4.

7. Proceed as in Hand-Dipping (page 51), Steps 1 through 7.

Molding and Decorating with Chocolate

Whether you are using small molds to make delicious bite-sized morsels or large forms for Easter, birthdays, Valentine's Day, or any holiday, having cleverly molded chocolates in your chocolate assortment will give it a more professional appearance. Tempered chocolate can be used for decorating Easter eggs and other molded forms, for piping initials with a pastry bag to identify filled candies, or for making filigree lace, chocolate "cigarettes," and leaves used to decorate cakes, pastries, and other desserts.

CHOCOLATE-MOLDING BASICS

1. Prepare chocolate, using the Easy-Method dipping mixtures (page 50) or Professional Dipping Chocolate (page 55). Chocolate will fall out of a mold with ease if it is properly tempered. Untempered chocolate is slow to harden and extremely difficult to remove. For this reason, it is important to follow the instructions for preparing the chocolate carefully.

2. The room should be free from steam, vapors, and drafts. Keep the temperature in the working area between 68°F. and 70°F.

3. The molds must be conditioned. When using plastic or metal molds for the first time, they should be washed by hand in warm water with a small amount of detergent. Rinse the molds thoroughly under running water, and wipe them with paper towels until the molding surface is dry and glossy. If you are using antique molds, do not wash them—ever. Wipe them with paper towels until the dark residue of age is removed. To reuse

molds after they have been filled with chocolate, run them under warm water and buff the molding surface to a high gloss. Do not refill the molds without cleaning off all residue from the previous molding, or your candies will have a dull finish.

Solid Molds

1. Molds should be clean, dry, and at room temperature.

2. Place molds on a smooth, level surface. You can pour the chocolate into large molds, but use a small spoon to fill individual molds. Whack the bottom of each mold soundly on a solid surface so the bubbles will rise to the top; then smooth the top with a wide spatula to even it off, or it will be difficult to get the chocolate out of the mold. Place the molds in the refrigerator for about 5 minutes or in a cool, dry room until firm.

3. To remove the candies from their molds, rap sharply against a hard surface to release, then turn them out onto a smooth surface. Store in single layers.

Hollow Shells: Method 1

1. Place the prepared molds on a smooth, level surface and fill them to the top with chocolate of a dipping consistency. Wait for the chocolate to become firm around the edges. The shell should be at least $\frac{1}{8}$ inch thick and the center should remain melted.

2. If you are using the Easy-Method dipping chocolate, very gently pour the melted center back into the pan. If you are using Professional Dipping Chocolate, pour the chocolate into a separate utensil because the coating will have to be retempered. Using the handle of a spatula, carefully tap the bottom of the shell, allowing any remaining melted chocolate to flow from the shell. Smooth excess chocolate from the rim. Shells must be cooled until firm before unmolding.

3. Place the hardened shells upside down on a smooth, soft surface. Very gently tap the bottom of the mold until the shell is released. If the shell does not drop out easily, and you have followed all the basic instructions, the chocolate has not cooled enough. Handle the chocolate with care to keep the warmth of your fingers from marring its smooth surface.

4. Fill the shells with mousse, ice cream, or fruits. Use a pastry tube to pipe the mixture into bite-size shells.

Hollow Shells: Method 2

1. Use a clean, dry pastry brush to coat the prepared molds with chocolate of a dipping consistency. Cool the chocolate briefly, but before it is completely set, brush on another layer. Repeat the cooling process. For very small shells, one coat of chocolate might be sufficient. If you are using very large molds, you will probably need to brush on several layers of chocolate. Bear in mind that a thin coating will be too fragile to support a heavy filling.

2. Cool for several hours, until firm. The shells may be placed in the refrigerator for about 5 minutes, longer if the shells are large. However, guard against overchilling, or you will have streaked and spotted shells.

Follow Steps 3 and 4 in Method 1.

Two-Piece Hinged Molds The professional way of molding Easter eggs, animals, and other unusual forms is to use a two-piece cast-aluminum mold. They come in a large range of sizes. If you are new at this, start with the smaller molds.

1. Condition the mold as discussed in Chocolate-Molding Basics, page 57.

2. Open the mold and lay it flat on a smooth, level surface. Fill one half of the mold to the very top with chocolate of a dipping consistency. With a spatula, smooth off any chocolate on the edges that might cause a molding line on the finished form. Close the two halves together and fasten tightly.

3. Shake the form gently to distribute the chocolate evenly inside the form. The center of the mold will be hollow. When the chocolate seems to have "set" inside the mold, place the form in a cool, dry place—but not in the refrigerator.

4. Wear white cotton gloves to remove the form from the mold so the warmth of your fingers does not mar the smooth surface. Remove the clamps and insert a dull knife around the rim of the mold. Rock the knife gently, first in one section of the mold, then in the other. You will feel the form being released. If the figure in the second section of the mold will not come loose, tap the surface gently. Let the figure drop out of the mold, holding it very close to a smooth, soft surface so it will not break. Do not be discouraged if you break the figure. Retemper the chocolate and try again.

To assemble hollow Easter eggs, fill a pastry tube with royal frosting, using your favorite recipe. Pipe a border around the seam line and decorate.

Foil Crinkle Cups These pretty foil cups are made especially for use in candy-making. They are sturdy enough to hold up when coated with chocolate, and can either be left on the chocolates, or peeled off before serving.

1. Have all the necessary ingredients measured and assembled in order of use. Since you will be working with small amounts, the chocolate will cool very fast, and you will need to work quickly.

2. Using a teaspoon, fill one cup about halfway. Swirl the cup to coat the sides and bottom, and immediately pour the melted chocolate back into the pan. Repeat with each cup, one at a time. Maintain the chocolate at dipping temperature (90°F.).

3. Place the chocolates on a baking sheet and set it in the refrigerator to firm for about 5 minutes.

4. Fill the cups with liqueur-soaked fruit, nuts, marzipan, fondant, or other filling.

5. To seal, spoon a layer of chocolate over the filled cup. Swirl the cup gently so the top is completely covered with chocolate. Place in a cool, dry place to firm.

Plastic Sheet Molds A sheet mold has a number of small indentations in it, similar to a muffin tin. Each mold in the sheet is filled using a teaspoon.

1. Condition the molds as in Chocolate-Molding Basics, page 57.

2. Place the sheet mold on a smooth, level surface and use a teaspoon to fill each cavity to the top with chocolate. Whack the sheet mold soundly on a solid surface so the bubbles will rise to the top. Let the chocolate set in the molds for about 5 minutes, to firm.

3. Turn the sheet mold over a baking sheet and allow the surplus chocolate to run out. Then turn the mold upright again and allow the chocolate to firm a little more. Use a wide spatula to level off the tops of the cavities.

4. Fill the cavities as in Step 5 for Foil Crinkle Cups (page 61).

5. To seal, spoon a layer of chocolate over each candy. Level off again with a wide spatula. Place in a cool, dry place to firm.

6. To unmold, turn the sheet over a smooth, soft surface and flex it to release chocolates.

CHOCOLATE GREETING CARDS

These are very easy to make! Wrapped in foil and carefully packaged, they can even be sent via the U.S. mail. Birthday, Mother's Day, and get-well messages are but a few of the personal greetings that can be expressed on a block of chocolate. Use tempered chocolate or pastel summer coating in paper cones to decorate and write your special message. Follow the instructions for molding solid chocolate forms (page 59) and for chocolate decorating (page 61). Chocolate greeting cards can be made in any size or shape. I use the lid of a metal box, measuring 6¾ inches by 4¼ inches and ⅝ inch deep.

CHOCOLATE-DECORATING BASICS

You will need to prepare dipping chocolate, using the Easy-Method dipping mixtures on page 50 or Professional Dipping Chocolate (page 55). The temperature of the chocolate must remain constant throughout the decorating process. If the chocolate is too warm, it will not retain the desired shape. If it is too cool, it will break apart and splinter.

Small Initials Use a classic script to pipe small initials. A chocolatier would consider it almost a sacrilege to overembellish a handmade chocolate. Use, for example, a script *A* for apricot, *C* for cherry, and *R* for raspberry.

1. Prepare the chocolates. The coating should be almost firm and at room temperature.

2. Make a paper cone triangle of high-quality parchment, tightened to a needle-sharp point. You may have to cut the point a teeny bit to allow the chocolate to flow. Fill the cone no more than one-third full of chocolate.

3. Hold the cone at a 45° angle as you would a pen. Test first by piping an initial onto waxed paper, then use a firm, steady hand to pipe the initial directly onto the chocolate-coated center.

Fine Lines, Scrolls, and Dots Use the same technique as for making initials. The size of the opening at the end of the parchment tube will depend on the desired width of the lines and the size of the dots you wish to make.

Thin Filigree Lace and Other Fragile Forms

1. Trace any shape you wish onto a paper pattern sheet. Tape this outline onto the bottom of an inverted baking sheet and cover with waxed paper.

2. Use the filled tube to outline any form from simple circles to elaborate filigree lace and butterflies.

3. Chill the designs until firm. Pull the waxed paper gently over the edge of the pan, separating it from the chocolate design. Handle as little as possible.

Chocolate "Cigarettes"

1. With a straight-edged metal spatula, spread the chocolate in a very thin layer on the bottom of an inverted baking sheet and chill for 10 to 15 minutes, or until it loses its shine and is firm but not hard.

2. Put the metal spatula under an edge of the chocolate and push it firmly down and away from you so the chocolate curls as it is pushed. If the chocolate becomes too soft to form curls, rechill it for several minutes.

3. Transfer the "cigarettes" to a baking sheet lined with waxed paper and chill until ready to use.

Chocolate Leaves

1. Pick or buy fresh leaves and wash and dry them thoroughly to remove spray and dust. Gardenia, lemon, and rose leaves are among the most attractive. *Caution:* Some leaves are toxic. If in doubt, check with your local nursery or florist.

2. Take a single leaf, and with the vein side down so the finished leaf will have distinct markings, pull it over the surface of the dipping chocolate in the pot, or paint the chocolate onto the leaf with a small pastry brush.

3. Remove any extra chocolate by gently tapping the leaf against the side of the pan. Then place the leaf, chocolate side up, on a baking sheet lined with waxed paper and put in the refrigerator to harden.

4. When the chocolate has hardened, just peel off the leaf. You'll have perfect chocolate "leaves" with the veins from a real leaf imprinted in the chocolate.

Chocolate Triangles

1. With a metal spatula, spread the chocolate to a depth of ⅛ inch on the bottom of an inverted baking sheet and chill until hard.

2. With a sharp knife, cut triangles that measure 1½ inches by 4 inches with a right angle. Rechill the chocolate until firm but not hard. Lift each triangle gently from the baking sheet with a spatula.

CHOCOLATE PAINTING

Y ou have probably seen painted chocolates displayed in candy boutiques at Easter, Christmas, and other holidays. They are very expensive, but, surprisingly enough, not difficult to make once you have mastered the simple techniques for tempering chocolate and molding solid chocolate forms.

Use indented molds like the Easter bunny, Santa Claus, Valentine hearts and flowers. The "painting" is done with contrasting shades of melted summer coating, and you will need a small artist's brush for each shade.

1. Review Chocolate-Molding Basics (page 57). The molds should be clean, dry, and at room temperature.

2. Melt the summer coating, chopped, in small jars submerged in warm—not hot—water, one for each color. Take care to keep the temperature of the coating under 120°F. It must remain fluid for intricate brushwork.

3. Color in the different areas of the mold as desired, keeping the brush within the indentations. Chill the mold in the refrigerator until the coating is no longer shiny, about 5 minutes.

4. Prepare the chocolate coating, using the Easy-Method mixtures (page 50) or Professional Dipping Chocolate (page 55).

5. Follow Steps 2 and 3 on page 59 for filling solid molds.

Chocolate
Temptations

People seem quite willing to pay outrageous prices for the exquisite chocolates that are displayed in select confectioneries. If you study the chocolates carefully you will discover that many can be recreated in your own kitchen, using the basic techniques in this book. Working with chocolate is not difficult. In no time at all you will be inventing marvelous new chocolate creations that are unique to you.

Dipping and molding fancy chocolates should not only nourish the spirit but should give you hours of fun as well. A gift of fine chocolates is perfect for Valentine's Day, Easter, Mother's Day, Chanukah, Christmas, or birthdays, and the gift becomes much more thoughtful if you make the chocolates yourself.

TRUFFLE-MAKING BASICS Consisting of a densely flavored combination of rich chocolate and other ingredients, truffles are French in origin. They are also among the easiest candies to duplicate in the home kitchen. The soft centers may be molded in irregular round shapes and rolled in cocoa to form the classic *les truffes aux chocolat,* or the centers may be shaped in a round ball, dipped in a thin coating of chocolate, and then rolled in cocoa, finely chopped nuts, flaked coconut, or crushed toffee bits. The final coating will disguise any flaws that result from dipping cooled centers into warm chocolate.

Truffles should be soft in the center and of a consistency described by one chocolatier as "almost melting on the tongue." The soft mixture can be somewhat tedious to shape in a form which will withstand the pressures of rolling and dipping.

Molding Truffle Centers

Method 1: Drop mixture by teaspoonfuls onto a baking sheet lined with waxed paper. Refrigerate until firm.

Method 2: Follow Method 1. After the truffles have firmed in the refrigerator, remove them and roll the irregular shapes into small (¾- to 1½-inch) balls. Refrigerate again until firm.

Method 3: Fit a pastry bag with a ½-inch (No. 7) plain tip. Spoon the truffle mixture into the bag. Pipe 1-inch truffles onto a baking sheet lined with waxed paper. Refrigerate until firm.

Method 4: Use a truffle scoop to drop perfectly formed round centers onto a baking sheet lined with waxed paper. Refrigerate until firm. A truffle scoop is a 1-inch miniature copy of an ice-cream scoop, made in Italy of quality stainless steel.

Coating Truffle Centers can be awkward, and it is helpful to be ambidextrous. If you are merely coating the fresh truffles in cocoa, there is not much of a problem.

Method 1: Sift the cocoa onto a baking sheet. Space the truffles on the cocoa so there will be room enough to gently roll the balls around until they are completely encased. The truffles will need to be refrigerated to retain freshness and shape. It may be necessary to roll them again in cocoa before serving.

Method 2: If you are dipping the truffles in chocolate before rolling them in coating, it helps to have a cooking partner do the coating for you. If you are right-handed, all the rolling and coating must be done with the left hand. My method is to fill small bowls with a selection of coatings (see recipe recommendations). With the right hand, put the chocolate-coated truffle into the coating; with your left hand, which should be free of chocolate, roll the truffle by tipping the bowl or pan around in a swirling motion. Pick up the finished truffle with the left hand and place it on a tray lined with waxed paper. Place in the refrigerator or in a cool place until firm.

Storing Truffles Truffles will stay fresh about 1 week in a cool room or the refrigerator.

CLASSIC FRENCH TRUFFLES

These truffles have all the qualities we love in chocolate. They are dark, rich, and dense—not light, fluffy, or overly sweet.

Use the highest-quality chocolate that you can find when making this recipe. (The less sugar added, the stronger and more chocolatey the flavor will be.) I recommend any of the following: Bissinger's (dark vanilla chocolate), Hershey's Special Dark Chocolate bar, Lindt Rod (bittersweet), Sarotti Plain Chocolate (semisweet), Suchard Bittra (bittersweet), and Tobler Tradition (bittersweet).

The French method is to begin with a *ganache,* a combination of chocolate and boiled cream.

Makes about 60 one-inch truffles

1 cup plus 1 tablespoon heavy cream
¼ cup (4 tablespoons) unsalted butter, cut in slivers
¾ pound (12 ounces) dark chocolate, chopped

1. Heat the cream and butter in a 2-cup saucepan and let simmer for 5 minutes. Set aside to cool.

2. Melt the chocolate in the top of a double boiler over hot, not simmering, water. Gradually blend the cooled cream mixture into the melted chocolate, stirring until smooth. The cooled cream and melted chocolate should be approximately the same temperature when mixed together.

3. Remove the mixture from the heat and cool to room temperature. Cover securely with plastic wrap and refrigerate overnight, or for at least 8 hours, to firm the mixture and ripen the flavors.

4. Follow the directions for molding and coating truffles in Truffle-Making Basics on page 67.

TRUFFLES GUADALAJARA In Step 1, remove the cream and butter mixture from the heat and stir in 2 teaspoons instant espresso coffee and ½ teaspoon ground cinnamon.

LIQUEUR-FLAVORED TRUFFLES Reduce the cream by 2 tablespoons. In Step 3, after the mixture has cooled, add 2 tablespoons of Kahlua, Frangelico, peppermint schnapps, fruit-flavored brandy, Cognac, bourbon, or dark rum.

CHOCOLATE ALMOND AND HONEY NOUGAT TRUFFLES

The buttery-rich chocolate flavor of these truffles more than justifies the expense of preparation. Use a bittersweet chocolate coating to contrast with the milk chocolate centers.

Makes 36 one-inch truffles

½ cup heavy cream
2 tablespoons unsalted butter, cut in slivers
3 three-ounce Toblerone Swiss milk chocolate bars with almond and honey nougat

1. Heat the cream and butter in a small saucepan until the mixture comes to a boil. Set aside to cool.

2. Melt the chocolate in the top of a double boiler over hot, not simmering, water. *Caution:* Do not heat the melted chocolate over 88°F., or the nougat bits will dissolve.

3. Remove the chocolate from the heat and gradually blend in the cooled cream, stirring until smooth. The cooled cream and melted chocolate should be approximately the same temperature when mixed together. Cool entire mixture to room temperature.

4. Cover securely with plastic wrap and refrigerate overnight, or for at least 8 hours, to firm the mixture and ripen the flavors.

5. Shape the chilled mixture into ½- to 1-inch balls for dipping in chocolate coating. The truffles may also be rolled in a final coating of cocoa or lightly roasted, finely ground almonds.

CHOCOLATE ALMOND BUTTER TRUFFLES

The subtle flavor of almond butter forms the base for these sensuous chocolate morsels.

Makes 25 one-inch truffles

2 squares (2 ounces) unsweetened chocolate
6 tablespoons unsalted butter
1½ cups confectioners' sugar (measure before sifting)
¾ cup almond butter
½ cup lightly roasted almonds, finely chopped (optional)

1. Melt the chocolate in the top of a double boiler over hot, not simmering, water.

2. Combine the melted chocolate, butter, confectioners' sugar, and almond butter in a mixing bowl or food processor. Blend the ingredients but do not overmix. When using a food processor, blend on low for a little less than 1 minute. Overmixing will make the centers too soft for dipping in chocolate. Stir in optional almonds.

3. Cover securely with plastic wrap and refrigerate several hours to firm the mixture and ripen the flavors.

4. Shape into ½- to 1-inch balls for dipping in chocolate coating. Truffles also may be rolled in a final coating of cocoa.

CHOCOLATE FILBERT TRUFFLES

It is necessary to remove the skins from the filberts (hazelnuts) in this recipe. See directions on page 14.

Makes 30 one-inch truffles

2 cups semisweet chocolate bits
1 square (1 ounce) unsweetened chocolate
1 cup filberts, lightly roasted and finely chopped
¾ cup sweetened condensed milk
⅛ teaspoon salt
1 teaspoon vanilla extract

1. Melt the chocolates in the top of a double boiler over hot, not simmering, water.

2. Remove from heat and stir in the filberts, condensed milk, salt, and vanilla. Blend with a wooden spoon until slightly thickened.

3. Cool for 5 minutes. The mixture should be firm enough to hold its shape. It may be necessary to chill it in the refrigerator. Shape into ½- to 1-inch balls for dipping in chocolate coating. Truffles may also be rolled in a final coating of cocoa.

CHOCOLATE MOUSSE TRUFFLES

This is a good recipe for beginners. The mixture is firm enough to be handled easily, and it is not necessary to roll the freshly dipped truffles in ground nuts or cocoa unless desired. The candies should dry with a nice glossy finish.

Makes 24 one-inch truffles

3 squares (3 ounces) unsweetened chocolate
⅓ cup unsalted butter
1¼ cups confectioners' sugar (sift before measuring)
4 large egg yolks
1 teaspoon vanilla extract

1. Melt the chocolate in the top of a double boiler over hot, not simmering, water.

2. Combine the butter and confectioners' sugar in a mixing bowl or food processor. Blend until smooth.

3. Blend in the egg yolks, one at a time.

4. Stir in the chocolate and vanilla.

5. Chill until the mixture is stiff. Shape into ½- to 1-inch balls for dipping in chocolate coating.

CHOCOLATE TRUFFLE CUPS

These are elegant little chocolate cups filled with a swirl of rich truffle paste.

Makes 60 to 80 truffle cups, depending on size of cup

Prepare the chocolate using Easy-Method mixtures (page 50) or Professional Dipping Chocolate (page 55). Follow the instructions for molding foil crinkle cups on page 61. Prepare the truffle mixture, using any recipe in this book.

1. Fit a piping bag with a medium-size open or closed star tube. Fold down the top of the bag to form a deep cuff. Spoon the soft truffle mixture into the bag until it is filled up to the cuff. Unfold the cuff and twist, pushing the truffle mixture down into the tube to eliminate air pockets.

2. Pipe the truffle mixture into the prepared chocolate shells until each is about two-thirds full. Then add a swirl of truffle mixture on top to finish each cup. Top the swirl with a roasted whole nut or candied violet, if desired. Let candies firm for about 30 minutes in the refrigerator. Serve at room temperature.

CHOCOLATE MOCHA TRUFFLES

Use premium-quality instant espresso and cocoa for a luscious creamy flavor.

Makes 36 one-inch truffles

2 teaspoons instant espresso coffee
½ cup boiling water
2 tablespoons unsalted butter
5 to 6 tablespoons Dutch-process cocoa
4 cups confectioners' sugar (measure before sifting)
½ teaspoon vanilla extract
¾ cup finely chopped walnuts

1. Combine the coffee and boiling water.

2. Combine the butter, cocoa, confectioners' sugar, and vanilla in a mixing bowl or food processor and blend until smooth.

3. Slowly add the coffee mixture and blend until smooth.

4. Stir in the walnuts. Chill until the mixture is stiff.

5. Shape into ½- to 1-inch balls for dipping in chocolate coating, and roll in additional cocoa if desired.

CHOCOLATE BUTTERCREME TRUFFLES

These butter-rich truffles not only appeal to your sense of taste, they nourish the spirit as well.

Makes about 75 one-inch truffles

½ pound (2 sticks) unsalted butter, at room temperature
4 squares (4 ounces) unsweetened chocolate, chopped
1 large egg, lightly beaten
1 teaspoon vanilla extract
1 pound (4¼ cups) confectioners' sugar (measure before sifting)

1. Melt half (1 stick) of the butter and the chocolate in a double boiler over hot, not simmering, water. Cool until slightly thickened.

2. Place the chocolate mixture in a mixing bowl or food processor. Blend in the remaining butter, egg, and vanilla. (Don't be alarmed at the appearance of the curdled mixture.)

3. Gradually add the sugar and continue mixing until light and fluffy.

4. Cover securely with plastic wrap and refrigerate for several hours to firm the mixture and ripen the flavors.

5. Shape into ½- to 1-inch balls for dipping in chocolate coating. Truffles may also be rolled in a final coating of nuts, coconut, or toffee bits.

WHITE CREME TRUFFLES

Be creative: use finely chopped dried fruits, nuts, and flavorings or liqueurs to give the white chocolate a refined and delicate flavor.

Makes 75 one-inch truffles

1 cup minus 1 tablespoon heavy cream
¾ pound (12 ounces) white chocolate, chopped
¼ pound (1 stick) unsalted butter
Flavoring or liqueur (see Variations below)
Dried fruits, or lightly roasted and finely chopped nuts (see Variations)

1. Heat the cream in a small saucepan and let simmer for 3 minutes. Set aside to cool.

2. Melt the chocolate and butter in the top of a double boiler over hot, not simmering, water.

3. Gradually blend the cooled cream into the chocolate-butter mixture. Remove from heat and cool to room temperature.

4. Add desired flavoring, liqueur, nuts, or dried fruits (see Variations).

5. Cover securely with plastic wrap. Refrigerate overnight, or for at least 8 hours, to firm the mixture and ripen the flavors.

6. Shape into ½- to 1-inch balls for dipping in dark or white chocolate coating. Coated truffles can then be rolled in cocoa, if desired.

VARIATIONS Add any of the following in Step 4:

½ teaspoon maple flavoring and 1 cup finely chopped walnuts
1 teaspoon almond flavoring and 1 cup lightly roasted, finely chopped almonds
½ cup finely chopped dried apricots and ½ cup lightly roasted, finely chopped pistachio nuts
2 tablespoons Frangelico and 1 cup lightly roasted, finely chopped filberts (hazelnuts)
2 tablespoons Grand Marnier and 2 tablespoons finely chopped orange peel

WHITE CHOCOLATE AND SUMMER COATINGS

White chocolate, not to be confused with white summer coating, is not really chocolate because it does not contain chocolate liquor. It does contain enough cocoa butter to give it a slightly chocolaty flavor, however, so it must be tempered in the same manner as real chocolate.

Summer coatings are compound coatings consisting of sugar, vegetable fats, milk solids, emulsifiers, fatty or nonfatty acids, flavorings, and sometimes cocoa and colorings. This product does not contain cocoa butter; therefore, it has a higher melting point than chocolate. Melted compound coatings are softer when they cool and firm, so they are ideal to use as coating for candy centers. Unlike chocolate, they are excellent to use in warm weather—hence their name, summer coatings.

EASY CHOCOLATE-COVERED CHERRIES

It is not necessary to double-dip these nonalcoholic confections, but you will need foil cups to hold the coated cherries.

Makes up to 200 candies

1. Prepare Chocolate Fondant (page 40).

2. Use Maraschino cherries with stems, as many as desired. Drain off the liquid and let the cherries stand on a rack to dry.

3. Pinch off small pieces of fondant, flatten them between your palms, and wrap around each cherry. Place the wrapped cherries in the refrigerator to firm for 3 to 4 hours. Remove 30 minutes before dipping in chocolate coating.

4. Dip the fondant-coated cherries into the chocolate, holding them by the stem. Deposit the coated cherry in a foil cup to firm and glaze over. Store in a cool, dry place—not the refrigerator.

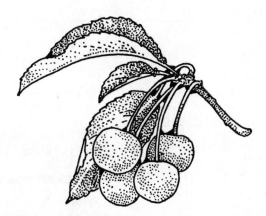

CHOCOLATE-COVERED CHERRY CORDIALS

Do not try this recipe until you are familiar with preparing Chocolate Fondant and have had some experience with chocolate dipping. Once you have mastered these you will be able to make these exquisite candies, fit for royalty.

You should make the candies in quantity (this recipe can easily be doubled), and it helps if you can work with an assistant. The recipe calls for a three-step process: (1) soak the cherries in liqueur overnight for flavor; (2) dip them in melted fondant; and (3) coat them with chocolate.

Makes about 40 cherries

1 pound prepared candied cherries (do not use Maraschino type)
brandy, kirsch, or rum to cover
confectioners' sugar for coating
1 ½ cups Chocolate Fondant, freshly made (page 40)
½ ounce grain alcohol, ½ ounce glycerine, ½ ounce 8% acetic acid (vinegar), and 1 ounce distilled water, mixed by a pharmacist*

prepared chocolate coating (use Easy-Method mixtures, page 50, or Professional Dipping Chocolate, page 55)

1. The night before you plan to make these cordials, prepare the cherries by rinsing them thoroughly under running warm water. This will remove the bitter almond taste. Shake off any excess water, place them in a jar, and cover with the brandy or other liquor. For a milder flavor, soak for only 3 to 4 hours. The cherries can be left in liqueur up to 3 weeks, if desired.

2. The next morning, drain the cherries thoroughly—but do not squeeze—and place them on a rack to dry. The fondant will not adhere to the cherries if they are damp.

3. After drying, roll the cherries in confectioners' sugar until they are completely coated, then place them in a strainer and lightly shake off the surplus sugar.

4. Melt the fondant in the top of a double boiler over simmering, but not boiling, water.

---

*In some states this compound may require a prescription from your doctor, due to the alcohol content. Only ½ teaspoon will be used. You can mix this yourself by substituting 100-proof vodka for the grain alcohol. And as a last resort you may use 1 ½ tablespoons of the liqueur left from soaking the cherries, in place of the chemical mixture. The fondant will not liquefy as readily if you use the soaking liqueur, but it will be quite soft.

5. Add ½ teaspoon of the grain alcohol mixture and stir until thoroughly blended.

6. Using a dipping fork or dinner fork, immediately dip the cherries in the fondant and place them on a tray. Place the tray in the refrigerator for a few minutes to firm.

7. Remove the fondant-coated cherries and dip them in the chocolate coating. This must be done immediately or the fondant will start to liquefy and run all over the tray. Unlike other dipping centers, these candies must be double-dipped to form a very strong coating for the liquid around the cherry. The first coat should be firm before the second is applied. The total liquefying process will take 12 hours. As the fondant liquefies it will settle to the bottom of the chocolate, and a thin layer of chocolate would not be strong enough to withstand the internal pressure of the liquid. (You can also prepare chocolate cups, page 61. Place the chocolate-coated cherry in the chocolate cup and seal the top with additional chocolate coating.)

8. Place the chocolate-coated cherries on waxed paper to dry and glaze over. Store them in a cool, dry place, but not in the refrigerator.

CHOCOLATE-COVERED PINEAPPLE CORDIALS
Substitute ½-inch cubes of candied pineapple for the cherries.

ORANGE TWIGS

These candied orange peel strips are coated with bittersweet chocolate.

Makes about 70 twigs

5 or 6 thin-skinned oranges
2½ cups granulated sugar, sifted
1 cup water
½ teaspoon cream of tartar
1 pound bittersweet chocolate, tempered for dipping

1. Score the oranges with a sharp knife in strips ½ inch across at the widest point, starting at the stem end. Cut the peel from the oranges and trim the ends to make twig-shaped pieces. Scrape most of the white pith from the peelings and discard.

2. Place the peels in a heavy 2-quart saucepan and cover with cold water. Bring to a boil and drain off the water. Repeat the boiling and draining two more times to remove the bitterness from the peels. Put the peels in a bowl and set aside.

3. Put 2 cups of sugar and the 1 cup of water in the pan and boil for 3 minutes. Stir in the peels and bring to a boil. Reduce the heat and simmer 45 minutes or until the peels are transparent.

4. Sift together the remaining ½ cup sugar and cream of tartar. Sift the mixture over the peels. Roll to coat thoroughly. Place the coated peels on a cooling rack and let stand at room temperature overnight.

5. Prepare dipping chocolate, using Easy-Method mixtures (page 50) or Professional Dipping Chocolate (page 55). Dip the peels in chocolate by hand or using small tongs. Shake off any excess chocolate and place on a waxed paper–lined baking sheet. Set in a cool place to firm.

HALF DIPS

These partially dipped candies work best when you use a firm, nonsticky center such as fudge or divinity.

Fudge Half Dips

1. Prepare any fudge recipe in this book. Cut the fudge into small bars, about ½ inch wide and 1 inch long. Brush off any crumbs on the pieces while cutting.

2. Prepare dipping chocolate, using the Easy-Method mixtures (page 50) or Professional Dipping Chocolate (page 55).

3. Hold one end of the bar and dip it into the melted chocolate. Shake off any excess chocolate. Place on a waxed paper–lined baking sheet to firm.

Divinity Half Dips (Black Bottoms)

1. Prepare divinity (page 42).

2. Drop the divinity from the tip of a teaspoon into small mounds. Immediately press a small pecan half onto the top of each mound. Cool until firm.

3. Prepare dipping chocolate, using Easy-Method mixtures (page 50) or Professional Dipping Chocolate (page 55).

4. Hold the divinity and dip the bottom into the melted chocolate, coating only the bottom half. Shake off any excess chocolate. Place on a waxed paper–lined baking sheet to firm.

COCONUT HAYSTACKS

These yummy coconut candies are lightly baked to a crisp, golden brown, then the bottom half is dipped in chocolate.

Makes 24 haystacks

5½ cups freshly grated coconut
1 cup granulated sugar, sifted
1 teaspoon vanilla extract
2 large eggs, well beaten
dipping chocolate

1. Preheat oven to 350°F.

2. Grate the coconut. This may be done in the food processor, following the manufacturer's directions.

3. Combine the coconut, sugar, and vanilla in a large mixing bowl and blend well. Add the eggs and mix thoroughly.

4. Pinch off a small amount of the mixture at a time and roll into balls the size of a walnut, then shape into cones about 1½ inches long.

5. Place the cones on parchment paper or on a waxed paper–lined baking sheet. Bake 15 minutes or until the tops are very lightly browned.

6. Place the baking sheet on a wet towel and remove the cones immediately with a wet spatula. Set on a wire rack to cool.

7. Prepare dipping chocolate, using the Easy-Method mixtures (page 50) or Professional Dipping Chocolate (page 55).

8. Hold the cone and dip the bottom into melted chocolate. Shake off any excess chocolate. Place on a waxed paper–lined baking sheet to firm.

CHOCOLATE PECAN TURTLES

I'd like to think these famous American candies were discovered accidentally by a confectioner who was left at the end of the day with a bit of soft caramel, some extra dipping chocolate, and an abundance of pecans. This recipe calls for approximately 1 pound of pecan halves and 4 cups of chopped or grated chocolate.

Makes about 48 candies

1. Prepare Soft Caramel (page 35).

2. Spread the pecan halves on a lightly oiled baking sheet, rounded side up. Using a teaspoon, drop warm caramel onto the pecan halves. The drops should be no more than 1 inch in diameter and not too close together.

3. When the caramel has cooled and set, lift out the turtle centers and place them on a cooling rack until firm.

4. Prepare dipping chocolate, using the Easy-Method mixtures (page 50) or Professional Dipping Chocolate (page 55).

5. Brush the underside of each cooled turtle lightly with chocolate coating, using a pastry brush or your finger. Cool until the chocolate is firm. Then turn the turtles over and spoon dipping chocolate over the top, covering the caramel completely. Let stand until the chocolate has firmed. (Although these candies can be eaten as soon as they harden, they taste even better if permitted to stand for 24 hours.)

CARAMEL PECAN LOGS

These confections are found almost everywhere candy is sold. It's so easy to make your own. The center of the log can be made with divinity or fondant, but I prefer the rich taste of chocolate fudge.

1. Prepare any chocolate fudge recipe in this book. Shape the fudge into finger-size rolls, or make one large roll. Cool until firm.

2. Prepare Soft Caramel (page 35).

3. Coat the rolls with warm caramel, using a small pastry spatula. After each roll is coated, immediately roll it in chopped pecans and press down so the nuts will adhere to the caramel. Cool until firm. Slice to serve.

MARICLAIRES

These are an adaptation of a popular Midwestern candy and can be dipped in milk or dark chocolate coating, making the finished product quite large. They are usually sold two to a small box.

Makes about 70 candies

1. Prepare Chocolate Fondant (page 40).

2. Shape the fondant into ¾-inch squares. Press each square into finely chopped pecans, coating all sides. Cool to firm.

3. Prepare dipping chocolate, using the Easy-Method mixtures (page 50) or Professional Dipping Chocolate (page 55).

4. Dip the candies and place them on a waxed paper–lined baking sheet to firm.

CHOCOLATE CARAMEL MINTS

These melt-in-your-mouth mints are so sinfully rich that people find them irresistible.

Makes 48 mints

1. Prepare Soft Caramel (page 35), but substitute ¼ teaspoon or more oil of peppermint for the vanilla.

2. Drop the warm caramel from the tip of a teaspoon onto a lightly oiled baking sheet. Hold the spoon close to the baking sheet for perfectly formed rounds, keeping them about ¾ inch in diameter. Cool to room temperature.

3. Prepare dipping chocolate, using the Easy-Method mixtures (page 50) or Professional Dipping Chocolate (page 55). Coat the rounds and place them on a waxed paper-lined baking sheet to firm.

ROCKY ROADS

These are easy to make with tempered chocolate. Use quality marshmallows like Kraft or Campfire. Lesser brands often contain too much artificial vanilla flavoring.

Makes about 1½ pounds

20 ounces milk dipping chocolate
3 cups miniature marshmallows
1 cup coarsely chopped walnuts

1. Line three small loaf pans with plastic wrap. Smooth out any wrinkles so the candy will have a smooth surface.

2. Prepare the dipping chocolate, using the Easy-Method mixtures (page 50) or Professional Dipping Chocolate (page 55).

3. Add the marshmallows and walnuts and stir until they are well coated with chocolate.

4. Spoon the mixture into the loaf pans and smooth the top surface. Chill in the refrigerator until firm. Remove from pan. Slice to serve.

LAYERED CANDIES

These elegant candies are composed of layers of contrasting flavors cut into small squares or rectangles. Then if you want to make them really fancy, the squares can be dipped in chocolate.

APRICOT-CHOCOLATE

1. Prepare Apricot Caramel mixture, page 36.

2. Prepare Chocolate Mousse Truffle mixture, page 72.

3. Spread the apricot mixture evenly on the bottom of an 8 x 8-inch pan lined with lightly oiled aluminum foil. Spread the chocolate mixture to an equal depth over the apricot mixture.

4. Cool slightly and cut into ¾-inch squares. Refrigerate until firm. Makes about 100 candies.

FUDGE-ALMOND-CARAMEL

1. Prepare any chocolate fudge recipe in this book.

2. Prepare ½ cup blanched almonds (page 14), lightly roasted and chopped.

3. Prepare Soft Caramel, page 35.

4. Press the fudge into a lightly oiled 8 x 8-inch pan. Press the almonds on top in an even layer. Spread a thin layer of warm caramel over the almonds.

5. Cool slightly. Cut into ¾- to 1-inch squares. Refrigerate until firm. Makes about 100 candies.

TWO-TONE MARSHMALLOWS

1. Prepare Chocolate Marshmallows (page 22) and Vanilla Marshmallows (page 23), one recipe each.

2. Lightly butter two 8 x 8 x 2-inch square pans and sprinkle them liberally with a mixture of 1 cup confectioners' sugar and 1 cup cocoa.

3. Spread half the chocolate marshmallow mixture in each pan. Smooth the top surfaces. Spread half of the vanilla marshmallow mixture over the chocolate mixture. Smooth the surfaces and sprinkle with more of the sugar-cocoa mixture. Place in the refrigerator for several hours to firm. Follow directions for Chocolate Marshmallows, Steps 7 through 10. Each pan makes 64 1-inch marshmallows.

CHOCOLATE MINT LAYERS

You will need two pots of tempered coating, one milk and the other dark chocolate.

Makes 81 1-inch candies.

1. Clean the sides of a smooth-surfaced metal pan by wiping with paper towels, but do not oil. The pan should be no larger than 9 x 9 inches or you will have trouble keeping the layers even.

2. Prepare two pots of tempered chocolate coating. Use the Easy-Method mixtures (page 50) or Professional Dipping Chocolate (page 55). You will need twice as much dark chocolate as milk chocolate.

3. Flavor the milk chocolate with oil of peppermint to taste. Or you can substitute tempered white chocolate, tinted pale green with paste food coloring (page 16).

4. Pour one half of the dark chocolate into the baking pan. Rotate the pan until the chocolate is in an even layer. Chill about 10 minutes, until slightly firm. Do not overchill, or the layers will not adhere to each other.

5. Pour the peppermint-flavored chocolate over the dark chocolate, making an even layer. Again, refrigerate for about 10 minutes.

6. Pour the remaining half of the dark chocolate over the second layer, making an even layer. Refrigerate until firm.

7. Turn out the mold over a soft towel. If the chocolate has firmed sufficiently, it will shrink and come out of the pan easily. If it is difficult to remove, chill for a while longer. Cut the chocolate into squares or rectangles with a large chef's knife or a pizza wheel.

CHOCOLATE PEANUT BUTTER CUPS

These are always a favorite. If you are making them in candy-store size (about 2½ inches across), you will need pleated paper or foil cups and mini muffin pans to hold them.

Makes 24 2½-inch cups

PEANUT BUTTER FILLING

¼ cup unsalted butter, softened
1½ cups confectioners' sugar, sifted (measure before sifting)
¾ cup creamy-style peanut butter

1. Combine butter, sugar, and peanut butter in a large mixing bowl and stir with a wooden spoon until blended. Do not use an electric mixer or food processor because over-mixing will cause the centers to be too soft and runny.

2. Using your fingertips, shape the mixture into small balls. (The size will depend on the size of the cups to be filled.) Place them on a waxed paper–lined baking sheet and store in a cool place.

ASSEMBLING CUPS

1. Prepare dipping chocolate, using the Easy-Method mixtures (page 50) or Professional Dipping Chocolate (page 55).

2. Using a small, dry pastry brush, coat the inside of the cups with the chocolate. Place the cups in a muffin pan so they will retain their rounded shape. Put the pan in the refrigerator for 10 minutes for the chocolate to firm, then brush on another coat of chocolate. Refrigerate again for 10 minutes.

3. With your fingertips press the peanut butter balls into the prepared chocolate cups. The cups should be about two-thirds full to allow enough space to cover the cup with chocolate. Return the muffin pan to the refrigerator for 20 minutes.

4. Fill the rest of each cup with chocolate. Rap gently to release air bubbles which might form on the surface, then return to the refrigerator for about 30 minutes. Remove the molds from muffin tin but leave the cases on.

CHOCOLATE ALMOND BUTTER CUPS

Substitute almond butter and ½ teaspoon almond extract for the peanut butter.

CHOCOLATE PRALINE CUPS

Praline is a lovely center to use for molded cups.

Makes 24 2½-inch cups

1 14-ounce can of sweetened condensed milk
2 cups confectioners' sugar, sifted (measure
    before sifting)
⅓ cup lightly roasted filberts (hazelnuts) or
    almonds, finely chopped
5 tablespoons cocoa (optional)
1 teaspoon vanilla extract

1. Preheat oven to 425°F.

2. Pour the sweetened condensed milk into an 8 x 4 x 4-inch loaf pan. Cover tightly with aluminum foil, and place in a shallow pan twice as large as the loaf pan. Pour in boiling water to measure halfway up the sides of the loaf pan. Bake 1 hour, or until the mixture is thick and lightly caramel-colored.

3. Remove the foil, cool to room temperature, then stir in the sugar, nuts, optional cocoa, and vanilla. Cover and place in a cool, dry place for several hours to blend the flavors.

4. Follow directions for assembling Chocolate Peanut Butter Cups (page 88), Steps 1 through 4.

DOUBLE-DECKER FUDGE

Makes about 1 ½ pounds

1 ½ cups lightly roasted pecans, walnuts, or filberts, finely chopped
1 ½ cups confectioners' sugar (sift before measuring)
1 large egg white
2 tablespoons dark rum or other favorite liqueur
1 ½ cups semisweet chocolate bits
1 square (1 ounce) unsweetened chocolate, chopped (optional)
¾ cup sweetened condensed milk
1 tablespoon unsalted butter

1. Combine the nuts, sugar, egg white, and rum in a bowl and mix well. Spread the mixture evenly on the bottom of an 8 x 8-inch pan lined with lightly oiled aluminum foil.

2. Melt the chocolates in the top of a double boiler over hot, not simmering, water. Stir in the milk and butter. Cook until thickened, about 5 minutes.

3. Pour the chocolate mixture over the nut mixture. Chill until firm.

4. Turn out of the pan and cut into ¾- to 1-inch squares.

Source Guide

The following companies will supply high-quality candy-making equipment and ingredients by mail order or will tell you where to purchase these items in your area. There is a charge for the Maid of Scandinavia catalog and the Wilton yearbook. Other listed sources supply complimentary brochures and catalogs. The chocolate distributers carry only their own brand and sell in large slab quantities; the suppliers carry many brands and sell in small quantities.

Albert Uster Imports, Inc.
8517 Grovemont Circle
Gaithersburg, MD 20877
Distributors of Carma chocolate

Ambrosia Chocolate Co.
1133 North Fifth St.
Milwaukee, WI 53203
Distributors of ambrosia

Amen
29 Ritchfield Ct.
Rockville, MD 20850
Distributors of Lenotre chocolate

Bissinger's
205 West Fourth St.
Cincinnati, OH 45202
Distributors of Bissinger's sweetened and unsweetened chocolate

California Almond Growers Exchange
P.O. Box 1768
Sacramento, CA 95808
Almond butter

The Chef's Catalog
3915 Commercial Ave.
Northbrook, IL 60062
Truffle scoop

De Choix Specialty Foods Co.
58-25 52nd Ave.
Woodside, NY 11377
Distributors of Callebaut sweetened and unsweetened chocolate

Donna Deane Inc.
10 Keith Way
Hingham, MA 02043
Distributors of Merckens chocolate

Ghirardelli Chocolate Manufactory
Ghirardelli Sq., 900 North Point
San Francisco, CA 94109
Distributors of Ghirardelli chocolate

Hilliard's Chocolate System, Inc.
275 East Center St.
West Bridgewater, MA 02379
Automatic chocolate tempering and melting machine

Home Craft Chocolate
P.O. Box 29, Dept. 711
Port Chester, NY 10573
Candy molds and forms

H. Roth and Son Paprika Co.
1577 First Ave.
New York, NY 10028
Fine chocolate supplier

J & M Cake Supplies
3810 Bloor St. West
Islington, Ontario, Canada M9B 6C2
Crinkle cups for candies

Kitchen Glamor Inc.
26770 Grand River Ave.
Redford, MI 48240
Crinkle cups for candies, flavoring extracts and oils

Madame Chocolate Inc.
1940-C Lehigh Ave.
Glenview, IL 60025
Fine chocolate supplier

Maid of Scandinavia
3244 Raleigh Ave.
Minneapolis, MN 55416
Candy box liners and padding, candy thermometer and chocolate tempering thermometer, cocoa butter, crinkle cups for candies, dipping fork, flavoring extracts and oils, fondant paddle, food colors (liquid, paste, and powder), candy molds and forms, summer (compound) coating, also a fine chocolate supplier

Rees Import Inc.
177-06 Rockaway Blvd.
South Ozone Park, NY 11420
Distributors of Lindt chocolate

Starbucks Coffee and Tea
4555 University Way NE
Seattle, WA 98105
Distributors of Guittard chocolate

Sterling Candy Company
60 Graphic Pl.
Moonachie, NJ 07074
Distributors of Suchard chocolate

Wilbur Chocolate Co.
48 North Broad St.
Lititz, PA 17543
Distributors of Wilbur chocolate

Wilton Enterprises, Inc.
833 West 115th St.
Chicago, IL 60643
Dipping fork, flavoring extracts and oils, food colors (liquid, paste, and powder), candy molds and forms, summer (compound) coating

Index

almond
  chocolate, and honey nougat
    truffles, 70
  chocolate bark, 54
  fudge-caramel, 86
almond butter chocolate
  crunch, 38
  cups, 88
  fudge, 31
  truffles, 71
Amaretto balls, 21
ambrosia, 39
apricot-chocolate layers, 86

baking soda, 13
balls
  Amaretto, 21
  Grand Marnier, 24
  orange, 24
  peanut rum, 21
bars, marshmallow, 23
boiled-sugar candies, 25–43
bourbon fudge clusters, 32
butter, 13

candied flowers, 16
candy, first, 23
candymaking, 7
candy thermometers, 9–10
  chocolate-tempering, 9
  cleaning, 10
  commercial, 9
  at high altitudes, 10
  for home use, 9
  reading, 10
  testing, 9–10
  testing without, 10
  using, 10

caramel
  apricot, 36
  chocolate, 34
  chocolate mints, 85
  chocolate pecan turtles, 83
  fudge-almond, 86
  pecan logs, 84
  soft, 35
caramelized sugar, 11
cherries
  cordials, chocolate-covered,
    78–79
  easy chocolate-covered, 77
chocolate, as ingredient, 13
chocolate candy, storing and
    freezing, 15
chocolate-dipping, 45–56
  basics, 47
  centers for, 47
  chocolate almond bark, 54
  chocolate-coated fruit, 51
  early technique for, 49
  easy-method, 49
  hand-dipping procedure, 51
  preparation of chocolate
    coating, 50–51
  professional, 55
"chocolate flavored," 20
chocolate specialty shops, 7
chocolate-tempering
    thermometers, 9
Christmas divinity, 43
Christmas fudge, 31
clusters, chocolate
  coconut-raisin, 20
  nut, 20
  orange-walnut, 20
cocoa, as ingredient, 13

coconut
  chocolate fudge, 31
  freezing, 15
  fresh, preparing, 15
  fudge, 19
  haystacks, 82
  raisin chocolate clusters, 20
  tinting, 15
  toasted, marshmallows, 23
  toasting, 15
coffee cream, 14
coffee mocha fondant, 41
cold-water stages, 10
colorings, food, 16
corn syrup, 13–14
cream
  heavy, 14
  light, 14
cream of tartar, 13
crème de menthe marshmallows, 23

decorating, 62–63
  basics, 62
  chocolate "cigarettes," 62
  chocolate leaves, 62–63
  chocolate painting, 63
  chocolate triangles, 63
  fine lines, scrolls, and dots, 62
  thin filigree lace and other
    fragile forms, 62
dipping forks, 11
divinity
  basics, 43
  chocolate, 42
  Christmas, 43
  coffee mocha, 43
  half dips, 81
  orange, 43

equipment, 9–11
evaporated milk, 14

filbert chocolate truffles, 72
firm-ball stage, 10
flavorings, 16
flowers, candied, 16
foil crinkle cups, 61
fondant
  basics, 41
  chocolate, 40
  coffee mocha, 41
  vanilla, 41
food colorings, 16
forks, dipping, 11
fruit, chocolate-coated, 51
fudge
  almond-caramel, 86
  bourbon clusters, 32
  chocolate, 30–31
  chocolate almond butter, 31
  chocolate coconut, 31
  chocolate fruit, 30
  chocolate mint, 19
  chocolate nut, 30–31
  chocolate peanut butter, 31
  Christmas, 31
  coconut, 19
  double-decker, 90
  half dips, 81
  marshmallow, 31
  royal chocolate, 29
  spirited, 19
fudge-almond-caramel layers, 86
fudge-making basics, 27–28
  professional method, 28

glucose, 13–14
Grand Marnier balls, 24
greeting cards, chocolate, 61

half dips
  divinity (black bottoms), 81
  fudge, 81
hard-ball stage, 10

hard-crack stage, 11
heavy cream, 14
honey, 14
Hotrays, 47

Kron, Tom, 7

layered candies, 86
  apricot-chocolate, 86
  fudge-almond-caramel, 86
  two-tone marshmallows, 86
logs, caramel pecan, 84

maple creams, chocolate, 39
mariclaires, 84
marshmallows
  candy bars, 23
  chocolate, 22
  crème de menthe, 23
  cutting and shaping, 23
  fudge, 31
  toasted coconut, 23
  two-tone, 86
  vanilla, 23
milk, 14
mint chocolate layers, 87
mints, chocolate caramel, 85
mocha
  chocolate truffles, 74
  coffee divinity, 43
  coffee fondant, 41
molasses, 14
molds, molding
  basics, 59
  hollow shells, 59–60
  plastic sheet, 61
  solid, 59
  truffle centers, 67
  two-piece hinged, 60–61

never-fail, 19
nuts
  blanching, 14
  chocolate fudge, 30–31
  chopping, 14

removing skins, 14
roasting, 14
storing or freezing, 14–15

orange
  balls, 24
  divinity, 43
  twigs, 80
  walnut chocolate clusters, 20

peanut butter
  chocolate cups, 88
  chocolate fudge, 31
  filling, 88
peanut rum balls, 21
pecan
  caramel logs, 84
  chocolate turtles, 83
praline, chocolate, 33
  cups, 89

rocky roads, 85
royal chocolate fudge, 29

Salton Hotrays, 47
saucepans, 9
soft-ball stage, 10
soft-crack stage, 10
sorghum, 14
source guide, 91–92
spatulas, 9
spirited fudge, 19
sugar
  caramelized, 11
  confectioners', 13
  granulated, 13
  light and dark brown, 13
  superfine, 13

temperature-controlled candies,
  25–43
temptations, chocolate, 65–90
toasted coconut marshmallows, 23
toffee, 37

truffles, 67–76
  basics, 67
  chocolate, cups, 73
  chocolate almond and butter, 71
  chocolate almond and honey
    nougat, 70
  chocolate almond butter, 71
  chocolate buttercrème, 75
  chocolate filbert, 72
  chocolate mocha, 74
  chocolate mousse, 72
  classic French, 69
  coating centers, 67–68
  Guadalajara, 69
  liqueur-flavored, 69
  molding centers, 67
  storing, 68
  white crème, 76

turtles, chocolate pecan, 83
two-tone marshmallows, 86

vanilla
  fondant, 41
  marshmallows, 23

whipping cream, 14
white chocolate, 76
white summer coatings, 76